Survey of Assessment Practices in Higher Education

Vincennes University
Shake Learning Resources Center
Vincennes, In 47591-9986

ISBN #: 1-57440-100-9   © 2008   Primary Research Group Inc.

Survey of Assessment Practices in Higher Education

TABLE OF CONTENTS

SURVEY PARTICIPANTS 4
LIST OF TABLES 5
COLLEGE DEMOGRAPHIC INFORMATION 21
COLLEGE DEMOGRAPHIC INFORMATION 21
SUMMARY OF MAIN FINDINGS 22
    SUMMARY CHAPTER 1: DEPARTMENTAL ASSESSMENT 22
    DEVELOPING AN ASSESSMENT PLAN 22
    ASSESSMENT PLAN 22
    ASSESSMENT OFFICE 22
    USE OF SOFTWARE TO AID IN ASSESSMENT 22
    SUMMARY CHAPTER 2: STANDARDIZED TESTING 23
    REMEDIAL COURSES 23
    PAYOUT FOR STANDARDIZED TESTING 23
    SUMMARY CHAPTER 3: ASSESSMENT OFFICE 24
    PERCENTAGE OF COLLEGES WITH AN ASSESSMENT OFFICE 24
    FULL TIME ASSESSMENT EMPLOYEES 24
    ASSESSMENT OFFICE SALARY RANGE 25
    ASSESSMENT OFFICE SIZE 25
    ANNUAL ASSESSMENT OFFICE BUDGET 25
    ASSESSMENT PROFESSIONALS WORKING OUTSIDE OF THE MAIN ASSESSMENT OFFICE 25
    SIZE OF THE BASIC INSTRUCTOR EVALUATION FORM 26
    SUMMARY CHAPTER 4: STUDENT ASSESSMENT OF INSTRUCTORS 26
    QUESTIONNAIRES 26
    IMPACT OF STUDENT ASSESSMENT QUESTIONNAIRES ON TENURE DECISIONS. 27
    IMPACT OF STUDENT FACULTY ASSESSMENT QUESTIONNAIRES ON THE HIRING AND RETENTION OF
    ADJUNCT INSTRUCTORS 27
    FORMATS USED FOR THE COMPLETION OF STUDENT ASSESSMENT QUESTIONNAIRES 28
    IMPACT OF STUDENT COURSE EVALUATIONS ON MERIT PAY INCREASES FOR INSTRUCTORS 29
    SUMMARY CHAPTER 5: EVALUATION OF ADJUNCT FACULTY 29
    COURSES TAUGHT BY ADJUNCT FACULTY 29
    METHODS OF EVALUATING ADJUNCT FACULTY 30
    POLICY ON DETERMINING THE EVALUATION OF ADJUNCT FACULTY 30
    THE EVALUATION OF ADJUNCT INSTRUCTORS 31
        The Use of Student Evaluation Forms in Evaluating Adjunct Instructors *31*
        The Use of Standardized Tests in Evaluating Adjunct Instructors *31*
        The Use of In Class Visits by Full-Time Professors in Evaluating Adjunct Instructors *31*
    EVALUATING INSTRUCTORS 32
        The Use of Student Evaluation Forms in Evaluating Full Time Instructors *32*
        The Use of Standardized Tests to Evaluate Learning in Chosen Majors in Evaluating Instructors ... *32*
        The Use of Standardized Tests Provided by Testing Companies to Obtain Results to Compare to
        National Data in Evaluating Instructors *32*
        The Use of In Class Visits by Full-Time Professors or Other Evaluators in Evaluating Instructors ... *33*
    SUMMARY CHAPTER 6: FACULTY INVOLVEMENT IN ASSESSMENT 33
    ROLE OF COLLEGE FACULTY IN DEVELOPING THE COLLEGE'S ASSESSMENT VEHICLES 33
    FACULTY VIEWS ON ASSESSMENT EFFORTS 33
    CENTERS TO DEVELOP FACULTY TEACHING SKILLS 34
    APPROXIMATE ANNUAL ASSESSMENT OFFICE SPENDING 34
    POLICY TO LINK INSTRUCTOR COMPENSATION TO DOCUMENTED INCREASES IN TEACHING
    EFFECTIVENESS 34
    SUMMARY CHAPTER 7: TUTORING 34
    TUTORING OR STUDENT LEARNING CENTER 34

Survey of Assessment Practices in Higher Education

Location of the Tutoring or Learning Center 34
Summary Chapter 8: Assessing Student Services 34
Summary Chapter 9: Assessment Environment 35
Summary Chapter 10: Curriculum Changes 35
Summary Chapter 11: Use of Benchmarking Data 35
The Purchase of Student Performance Benchmarking Data 35
Colleges that use ZOOMERANG 35
Colleges that use WEAVEONLINE 35
Colleges that use SURVEYMONKEY 35
Colleges that use WEBSURVEYOR 35
Colleges that use STUDENTVOICE 36
Colleges that use KEY SURVEY 36
Colleges that use SURVEY TRACKER 36
Colleges that use SNAP 36
Colleges that use FLASHLIGHT ONLINE 36
Colleges that use ULTIMATE SURVEY 36
Summary Chapter 12: Use of Consultants and Services 36
Spending on Outside Consultants and Services Related to Assessment 36
Conferences Devoted to Assessment that Administrators Attended in the Past Year 37
Summary Chapter 13: Post Graduate Assessment 37
Colleges with a Post Graduate Assessment Program 37
Interviews of Students Who Graduate 37
Interviews of Students Who Transfer Out of College 37
Interviews of Students Who Drop Out of College 38
Number of Exit Interviews for Graduating Students 38
Exit Interviews Conducted With Students Who Left the College For Any Reason 38
Compensation for Students That Take Exit Interviews 38

CHAPTER 1: DEPARTMENTAL ASSESSMENT 39

CHAPTER 2: STANDARDIZED TESTING 51

CHAPTER 3: ASSESSMENT OFFICE 59

CHAPTER 4: STUDENT ASSESSMENT OF INSTRUCTORS 67

CHAPTER 5: EVALUATION OF ADJUNCT FACULTY 73

CHAPTER 6: FACULTY INVOLVEMENT IN ASSESSMENT 82

CHAPTER 7: TUTORING 88

CHAPTER 8: ASSESSING STUDENT SERVICES 90

CHAPTER 9: ASSESSMENT ENVIRONMENT 91

CHAPTER 10: CURRICULUM CHANGES 92

CHAPTER 11: USE OF BENCHMARKING DATA 94

CHAPTER 12: USE OF CONSULTANTS AND SERVICES 103

CHAPTER 13: POST GRADUATION ASSESSMENT 106

CHAPTER 14: ASSESSING ASSESSMENT 113

OTHER REPORTS FROM PRIMARY RESEARCH GROUP, INC. 117

Survey of Assessment Practices in Higher Education

Survey Participants

Amarillo College
Andrews University
Arizona State University
Auburn University (Main Campus)
Bethel University
Brookdale Community College
Brookhaven College
C.W. Post Campus of Long Island University
California State University, East Bay
Capella University
Chicago State University
Clearwater Christian College
Colegio Universitario de San Juan
College of Charleston
College of the Mainland
College of Wooster
Cornerstone University
Crafton Hills College
CSU Sacramento
Durham Technical Community College
East Tennessee State University
El Centro College
Elon U
Florida Community College at Jacksonville
Florida Gulf Coast University
Fort Lewis College
Gallaudet University
Hostos Community College
Hunter College, CUNY
Huston-Tillotson University
Illinois State University
Indiana University Kokomo
Indiana University-Purdue University Fort Wayne
Indiana Wesleyan University
Ivy Tech Community College
James Madison University
Lake Forest College
Lesley University
Louisiana State University
Malaspina University-College
Marquette University
Mercyhurst College
Middle Tennessee State University
Mount Union College
Mount Vernon Nazarene University
North Carolina State University
Northern Illinois University
Oakland University
Occidental College
Paul Smiths College
Radford University

Rich Mountain Community College
Rockford College
Saint Mary's University of Minnesota
Sam Houston State University
Seton Hall University
Sprott School of Business, Carleton University
St. Bonaventure University
Tacoma Community College
The University of Texas at Tyler
Tri-State University
University of California, Santa Barbara
University of North Carolina, Wilmington
University of Delaware
University of Evansville
University of Mobile
University of Nebraska College of Medicine
University of New Hampshire
University of North Dakota
University of St. Thomas
University of the Sciences in Philadelphia
University of Toledo
University of Virginia
University of Toledo
University of Texas, Austin
University of Wisconsin-La Crosse
Walsh University
Warren Wilson College
Washington State University
Wayne State College
West Texas A&M University
Western Carolina University
William Penn

Survey of Assessment Practices in Higher Education

List of Tables

Table 1.1: Percentage of colleges in the sample that require that academic departments develop an assessment plan identifying key concepts and ideas that students should master 39

Table 1.2: Percentage of colleges in the sample that require that academic departments develop an assessment plan identifying key concepts and ideas that students should master, Broken Out by Type of College 39

Table 1.3: Percentage of colleges in the sample that require that academic departments develop an assessment plan identifying key concepts and ideas that students should master, Broken Out by Public or Private Institutional Status 39

Table 1.4: Percentage of colleges in the sample that require that academic departments develop an assessment plan identifying key concepts and ideas that students should master, Broken Out by Full time equivalent enrollment 39

Table 1.5: Mean, Median, Minimum and Maximum percentage of the major departments in the college that have developed a detailed assessment plan 40

Table 1.6: Mean, Median, Minimum and Maximum percentage of the major departments in the college that have developed a detailed assessment plan, Broken Out by Type of College 40

Table 1.7: Mean, Median, Minimum and Maximum percentage of the major departments in the college that have developed a detailed assessment plan, Broken Out by Public or Private Institutional Status 40

Table 1.8: Mean, Median, Minimum and Maximum percentage of the major departments in the college that have developed a detailed assessment plan, Broken Out by Full time equivalent enrollment 40

Table 1.9: Percentage of college assessment offices (or other office entrusted with this task) that communicate with academic departments through designated assessment coordinators in the various academic departments 41

Table 1.10: Percentage of college assessment offices (or other office entrusted with this task) that communicate with academic departments through designated assessment coordinators in the various academic departments, Broken Out by Type of College 41

Table 1.11: Percentage of college assessment offices (or other office entrusted with this task) that communicate with academic departments through designated assessment coordinators in the various academic departments, Broken Out by Public or Private Institutional Status 41

Table 1.12: Percentage of college assessment offices (or other office entrusted with this task) that communicate with academic departments through designated assessment coordinators in the various academic departments, Broken Out by Full time equivalent enrollment 41

Table 1.13: Percentage of Colleges in the Sample that use the Assessment Package ACT 42

Table 1.14: Percentage of Colleges in the Sample that use the Assessment Package ACT, Broken Out by Type of College 42

Table 1.15: Percentage of Colleges in the Sample that use the Assessment Package ACT, Broken Out by Public or Private Institutional Status 42

Table 1.16:   Percentage of Colleges in the Sample that use the Assessment Package ACT, Broken Out by Full Time Equivalent Enrollment 42
Table 1.17:   Percentage of Colleges in the Sample that use the Assessment Package Accuplacer   42
Table 1.18:   Percentage of Colleges in the Sample that use the Assessment Package Accuplacer, Broken Out by Public or Private Institutional Status 43
Table 1.19:   Percentage of Colleges in the Sample that use the Assessment Package Accuplacer, Broken Out by Type of College 43
Table 1.20:   Percentage of Colleges in the Sample that use the Assessment Package Accuplacer, Broken Out by Full Time Equivalent Enrollment 43
Table 1.21:   Percentage of Colleges in the Sample that use the Assessment Package COMPASS   43
Table 1.22:   Percentage of Colleges in the Sample that use the Assessment Package COMPASS, Broken Out by Type of College 43
Table 1.23:   Percentage of Colleges in the Sample that use the Assessment Package COMPASS, Broken Out by Public or Private Institutional Status 44
Table 1.24:   Percentage of Colleges in the Sample that use the Assessment Package COMPASS, Broken Out by Full Time Equivalent Enrollment 44
Table 1.25:   Percentage of Colleges that Administer the Mathematics Section of COMPASS to incoming Freshmen 44
Table 1.26:   Percentage of Colleges that Administer the Mathematics Section of COMPASS to incoming Freshmen, Broken Out by Type of College 44
Table 1.27:   Percentage of Colleges that Administer the Mathematics Section of COMPASS to incoming Freshmen, Broken Out by Public or Private Institutional Status   44
Table 1.28:   Percentage of Colleges that Administer the Mathematics Section of COMPASS to incoming Freshmen, Broken Out by Full Time Equivalent Enrollment ... 45
Table 1.29:   Percentage of Colleges that Administer the Reading Section of COMPASS to incoming Freshmen 45
Table 1.30:   Percentage of Colleges that Administer the Reading Section of COMPASS to incoming Freshmen, Broken Out by Type of College 45
Table 1.31:   Percentage of Colleges that Administer the Reading Section of COMPASS to incoming Freshmen, Broken Out by Public or Private Institutional Status   45
Table 1.32:   Percentage of Colleges that Administer the Reading Section of COMPASS to incoming Freshmen, Broken Out by Full Time Equivalent Enrollment ... 45
Table 1.33:   Percentage of Colleges in the sample that Administer the Writing Section of COMPASS to incoming Freshmen 46
Table 1.34:   Percentage of Colleges in the sample that Administer the Writing Section of COMPASS to incoming Freshmen, Broken Out by Type of College 46
Table 1.35:   Percentage of Colleges in the sample that Administer the Writing Section of COMPASS to incoming Freshmen, Broken Out by Public or Private Institutional Status   46
Table 1.36:   Percentage of Colleges in the sample that Administer the Writing Section of COMPASS to incoming Freshmen, Broken Out by Full Time Equivalent Enrollment 46
Table 1.37:   Percentage of Colleges in the Sample that have ever used the NSSE 46

Table 1.38: Percentage of Colleges in the Sample that have ever used the NSSE, Broken Out by Type of College 47
Table 1.39: Percentage of Colleges in the Sample that have ever used the NSSE, Broken Out by Public or Private Institutional Status 47
Table 1.40: Percentage of Colleges in the Sample that have ever used the NSSE, Broken Out by Full Time Equivalent Enrollment 47
Table 1.41: Percentage of Colleges in the Sample that have ever used the HERI 47
Table 1.42: Percentage of Colleges in the Sample that have ever used the HERI, Broken Out by Type of College 47
Table 1.43: Percentage of Colleges in the Sample that have ever used the HERI, Broken Out by Public or Private Institutional Status 48
Table 1.44: Percentage of Colleges in the Sample that have ever used the HERI, Broken Out by Full Time Equivalent Enrollment 48
Table 1.45: Percentage of Colleges in the Sample that have ever used data from Educational Benchmarking, Inc. 48
Table 1.46: Percentage of Colleges in the Sample that have ever used data from Educational Benchmarking, Inc., Broken Out by Type of College 48
Table 1.47: Percentage of Colleges in the Sample that have ever used data from Educational Benchmarking, Inc., Broken Out by Public or Private Institutional Status .. 48
Table 1.48: Percentage of Colleges in the Sample that have ever used data from Educational Benchmarking, Inc., Broken Out by Full Time Equivalent Enrollment 49
Table 1.49: Percentage of Colleges in the Sample that have ever used the Center for Education Assessment 49
Table 1.50: Percentage of Colleges in the Sample that have ever used the Center for Education Assessment, Broken Out by Type of College 49
Table 1.51: Percentage of Colleges in the Sample that have ever used the Center for Education Assessment, Broken Out by Public or Private Institutional Status 49
Table 1.52: Percentage of Colleges in the Sample that have ever used the Center for Education Assessment, Broken Out by Full Time Equivalent Enrollment 49
Table 1.53: Percentage of Colleges in the Sample that have ever used Chalk & Wire EPortfolio   50
Table 1.54: Percentage of Colleges in the Sample that have ever used Chalk & Wire Eportfolio, Broken Out by Type of College 50
Table 1.55: Percentage of Colleges in the Sample that have ever used Chalk & Wire Eportfolio, Broken Out by Public or Private Institutional Status 50
Table 1.56: Percentage of Colleges in the Sample that have ever used Chalk & Wire Eportfolio, Broken Out by Full Time Equivalent Enrollment 50
Table 2.1: Percentage of Colleges in the Sample that offer remedial or developmental courses in WRITING for students who do not perform well enough on standardized tests to take the normal college curriculum 51
Table 2.2: Percentage of Colleges in the Sample that offer remedial or developmental courses in WRITING for students who do not perform well enough on standardized tests to take the normal college curriculum, Broken Out by Type of College 51
Table 2.3: Percentage of Colleges in the Sample that offer remedial or developmental courses in WRITING for students who do not perform well enough on standardized tests

to take the normal college curriculum, Broken Out by Public or Private Institutional Status   51

Table 2.4:   Percentage of Colleges in the Sample that offer remedial or developmental courses in WRITING for students who do not perform well enough on standardized tests to take the normal college curriculum, Broken Out by Full Time Equivalent Enrollment   51

Table 2.5:   Percentage of Colleges in the Sample that offer remedial or developmental courses in STUDY SKILLS for students who do not perform well enough on standardized tests to take the normal college curriculum 52

Table 2.6:   Percentage of Colleges in the Sample that offer remedial or developmental courses in STUDY SKILLS for students who do not perform well enough on standardized tests to take the normal college curriculum, Broken Out by Type of College   52

Table 2.7:   Percentage of Colleges in the Sample that offer remedial or developmental courses in STUDY SKILLS for students who do not perform well enough on standardized tests to take the normal college curriculum, Broken Out by Public or Private Institutional Status.. 52

Table 2.8:   Percentage of Colleges in the Sample that offer remedial or developmental courses in STUDY SKILLS for students who do not perform well enough on standardized tests to take the normal college curriculum, Broken Out by Full Time Equivalent Enrollment.. 52

Table 2.9:   Percentage of Colleges in the Sample that offer remedial or developmental courses in ENGLISH AS A SECOND LANGUAGE for students who do not perform well enough on standardized tests to take the normal college curriculum 53

Table 2.10:   Percentage of Colleges in the Sample that offer remedial or developmental courses in ENGLISH AS A SECOND LANGUAGE for students who do not perform well enough on standardized tests to take the normal college curriculum, Broken Out by Type of College 53

Table 2.11:   Percentage of Colleges in the Sample that offer remedial or developmental courses in ENGLISH AS A SECOND LANGUAGE for students who do not perform well enough on standardized tests to take the normal college curriculum, Broken Out by Public or Private Institutional Status 53

Table 2.12:   Percentage of Colleges in the Sample that offer remedial or developmental courses in ENGLISH AS A SECOND LANGUAGE for students who do not perform well enough on standardized tests to take the normal college curriculum, Broken Out by Full Time Equivalent Enrollment 53

Table 2.13:   Percentage of Colleges in the Sample that offer remedial or developmental courses in MATHEMATICS for students who do not perform well enough on standardized tests to take the normal college curriculum 54

Table 2.14:   Percentage of Colleges in the Sample that offer remedial or developmental courses in MATHEMATICS for students who do not perform well enough on standardized tests to take the normal college curriculum, Broken Out by Type of College   54

Table 2.15:   Percentage of Colleges in the Sample that offer remedial or developmental courses in MATHEMATICS for students who do not perform well enough on standardized tests to take the normal college curriculum, Broken Out by Public or Private Institutional Status 54

Table 2.16:   Percentage of Colleges in the Sample that offer remedial or developmental courses in MATHEMATICS for students who do not perform well enough on standardized tests to take the normal college curriculum, Broken Out by Full Time Equivalent Enrollment 54

Table 2.17:   Percentage of Colleges in the Sample that offer remedial or developmental courses in INFORMATION/COMPUTER LITERACY for students who do not perform well enough on standardized tests to take the normal college curriculum 55

Table 2.18:   Percentage of Colleges in the Sample that offer remedial or developmental courses in INFORMATION/COMPUTER LITERACY for students who do not perform well enough on standardized tests to take the normal college curriculum, Broken Out by Type of College 55

Table 2.19:   Percentage of Colleges in the Sample that offer remedial or developmental courses in INFORMATION/COMPUTER LITERACY for students who do not perform well enough on standardized tests to take the normal college curriculum, Broken Out by Public or Private Institutional Status 55

Table 2.20:   Percentage of Colleges in the Sample that offer remedial or developmental courses in INFORMATION/COMPUTER LITERACY for students who do not perform well enough on standardized tests to take the normal college curriculum, Broken Out by Full Time Equivalent Enrollment 55

Table 2.21:   Mean, Median, Minimum and Maximum amount that colleges in the sample spent to pay students to take standardized tests that are primarily used within the college to aid it in its assessment efforts in $U.S. 56

Table 2.22:   Mean, Median, Minimum and Maximum amount that colleges in the sample spent to pay students to take standardized tests that are primarily used within the college to aid it in its assessment efforts, in $U.S., Broken Out by Type of College 56

Table 2.23:   Mean, Median, Minimum and Maximum amount that colleges in the sample spent to pay students to take standardized tests that are primarily used within the college to aid it in its assessment efforts in $U.S., Broken Out by Public or Private Institutional Status 56

Table 2.24:   Mean, Median, Minimum and Maximum amount that colleges in the sample spent to pay students to take standardized tests that are primarily used within the college to aid it in its assessment efforts in $U.S., Broken Out by Full Time Equivalent Enrollment   56

Table 2.25:   Percentage of colleges sampled that offer a higher rate of pay or reward to students that score higher on standardized assessment tests, on the theory that this encourages full student effort 57

Table 2.26:   Percentage of colleges sampled that offer a higher rate of pay or reward to students that score higher on standardized assessment tests, on the theory that this encourages full student effort, Broken Out by Type of College 57

Table 2.27:   Percentage of colleges sampled that offer a higher rate of pay or reward to students that score higher on standardized assessment tests, on the theory that this encourages full student effort, Broken Out by Public or Private Institutional Status 57

Survey of Assessment Practices in Higher Education

Table 2.28: Percentage of colleges sampled that offer a higher rate of pay or reward to students that score higher on standardized assessment tests, on the theory that this encourages full student effort, Broken Out by Full Time Equivalent Enrollment 58

Table 3.2: Percentage of colleges that have an office of assessment or similar office or department that primarily devotes itself to assessment 59

Table 3.3: Percentage of colleges that have an office of assessment or similar office or department that primarily devotes itself to assessment, Broken Out by Type of College 59

Table 3.4: Percentage of colleges that have an office of assessment or similar office or department that primarily devotes itself to assessment, Broken Out by Public or Private Institutional Status 59

Table 3.5: Percentage of colleges that have an office of assessment or similar office or department that primarily devotes itself to assessment, Broken Out by Full Time Equivalent Enrollment 60

Table 3.6: Mean, Median, Minimum and Maximum Number of Full Time Employees in the sample college's office of assessment, or similar office that is primarily devoted to this function   60

Table 3.7: Mean, Median, Minimum and Maximum Number of Full Time Employees in the sample college's office of assessment, or similar office that is primarily devoted to this function, Broken Out by Type of College 60

Table 3.8: Mean, Median, Minimum and Maximum Number of Full Time Employees in the sample college's office of assessment, or similar office that is primarily devoted to this function, Broken Out by Public or Private Institutional Status 60

Table 3.9: Mean, Median, Minimum and Maximum Number of Full Time Employees in the sample college's office of assessment, or similar office that is primarily devoted to this function, Broken Out by Full Time Equivalent Enrollment 61

Table 3.10: Annual salary range for the highest ranking assessment officer 61

Table 3.11: Annual salary range for the highest ranking assessment officer, Broken Out by Type of College 61

Table 3.12: Annual salary range for the highest ranking assessment officer, Broken Out by Public or Private Institutional Status 61

Table 3.13: Annual salary range for the highest ranking assessment officer, Broken Out by Full Time Equivalent Enrollment 62

Table 3.14: Mean, Median, Minimum and Maximum size of college assessment office for colleges in the sample, in square feet 62

Table 3.15: Mean, Median, Minimum and Maximum size of college assessment office for colleges in the sample, in square feet, Broken Out by Type of College 62

Table 3.16: Mean, Median, Minimum and Maximum size of college assessment office for colleges in the sample, in square feet, Broken Out by Public or Private Institutional Status   62

Table 3.17: Mean, Median, Minimum and Maximum size of college assessment office for colleges in the sample, in square feet, Broken Out by Full Time Equivalent Enrollment   63

Table 3.18: Mean, Median, Minimum and Maximum annual budget, for colleges in the sample, of the assessment office, including salaries and overhead (in $U.S.) 63

Survey of Assessment Practices in Higher Education

Table 3.19:   Mean, Median, Minimum and Maximum annual budget, for colleges in the sample, of the assessment office, including salaries and overhead, Broken Out by Type of College 63

Table 3.20:   Mean, Median, Minimum and Maximum annual budget, for colleges in the sample, of the assessment office, including salaries and overhead., Broken Out by Public or Private Institutional Status 63

Table 3.21:   Mean, Median, Minimum and Maximum annual budget, for colleges in the sample, of the assessment office, including salaries and overhead, Broken Out by Full Time Equivalent Enrollment 64

Table 3.22:   Mean, Median, Minimum and Maximum number of assessment professionals working in other offices outside of the main college assessment office..... 64

Table 3.23:   Mean, Median, Minimum and Maximum number of assessment professionals working in other offices outside of the main college assessment office, Broken Out by Type of College 64

Table 3.24:   Mean, Median, Minimum and Maximum number of assessment professionals working in other offices outside of the main college assessment office, Broken Out by Public or Private Institutional Status 64

Table 3.25:   Mean, Median, Minimum and Maximum number of assessment professionals working in other offices outside of the main college assessment office, Broken Out by Full Time Equivalent Enrollment 65

Table 3.26:   Mean, Median, Minimum and Maximum number of questions on the basic instructor evaluation form given to students 65

Table 3.27:   Mean, Median, Minimum and Maximum number of questions on the basic instructor evaluation form given to students, Broken Out by Type of College 65

Table 3.28:   Mean, Median, Minimum and Maximum number of questions on the basic instructor evaluation form given to students, Broken Out by Public or Private Institutional Status   65

Table 3.29:   Mean, Median, Minimum and Maximum number of questions that the basic instructor evaluation form given to students, Broken Out by Full Time Equivalent Enrollment   66

Table 4.1:   Description of college's policies towards questionnaires for student assessment of instructors 67

Table 4.2:   Description of college's policies towards questionnaires for student assessment of instructors, Broken Out by Type of College 67

Table 4.3:   Description of college's policies towards questionnaires for student assessment of instructors, Broken Out by Public or Private Institutional Status 67

Table 4.4:   Description of college's policies towards questionnaires for student assessment of instructors, Broken Out by Full Time Equivalent Enrollment 68

Table 4.5:   Description of the impact of student faculty assessment questionnaires on tenure decisions 68

Table 4.6:   Description of the impact of student faculty assessment questionnaires on tenure decisions, Broken Out by Type of College 68

Table 4.7:   Description of the impact of student faculty assessment questionnaires on tenure decisions, Broken Out by Public or Private Institutional Status 68

Table 4.8:   Description of the impact of student faculty assessment questionnaires on tenure decisions, Broken Out by Full Time Equivalent Enrollment 69

Table 4.9: Description of the impact of student faculty assessment questionnaires on retention decisions regarding ADJUNCT instructors 69
Table 4.10: Description of the impact of student faculty assessment questionnaires on retention decisions regarding ADJUNCT instructors, Broken Out by Type of College... 69
Table 4.11: Description of the impact of student faculty assessment questionnaires on retention decisions regarding ADJUNCT instructors, Broken Out by Public or Private Institutional Status 69
Table 4.12: Description of the impact of student faculty assessment questionnaires on retention decisions regarding ADJUNCT instructors, Broken Out by Full Time Equivalent Enrollment 70
Table 4.13: Description of formats used for the completion of student assessment questionnaires 70
Table 4.14: Description of formats used for the completion of student assessment questionnaires, Broken Out by Type of College 70
Table 4.15: Description of formats used for the completion of student assessment questionnaires, Broken Out by Public or Private Institutional Status 70
Table 4.16: Description of formats used for the completion of student assessment questionnaires, Broken Out by Full Time Equivalent Enrollment 71
Table 4.17: Description of the impact of student course evaluations on merit pay increases for instructors 71
Table 4.18: Description of the impact of student course evaluations on merit pay increases for instructors, Broken Out by Type of College 71
Table 4.19: Description of the impact of student course evaluations on merit pay increases for instructors, Broken Out by Public or Private Institutional Status 71
Table 4.20: Description of the impact of student course evaluations on merit pay increases for instructors, Broken Out by Full Time Equivalent Enrollment 72
Table 5.1: Mean, Median, Minimum and Maximum percentage of courses taught by adjunct faculty 73
Table 5.2: Mean, Median, Minimum and Maximum percentage of courses taught by adjunct faculty, Broken Out by Type of College 73
Table 5.3: Mean, Median, Minimum and Maximum percentage of courses taught by adjunct faculty, Broken Out by Public or Private Institutional Status 73
Table 5.4: Mean, Median, Minimum and Maximum percentage of courses taught by adjunct faculty, Broken Out by Full Time Equivalent Enrollment 73
Table 5.5: Description of the method for evaluating adjunct faculty 74
Table 5.6: Description of the method for evaluating adjunct faculty, Broken Out by Type of College 74
Table 5.7: Description of the method for evaluating adjunct faculty, Broken Out by Public or Private Institutional Status 74
Table 5.8: Description of the method for evaluating adjunct faculty, Broken Out by Full Time Equivalent Enrollment 74
Table 5.9: Description of college's policy towards determining the evaluation of ADJUNCT instructors 75
Table 5.10: Description of college's policy towards determining the evaluation of ADJUNCT instructors, Broken Out by Type of College 75

Survey of Assessment Practices in Higher Education

Table 5.11: Description of college's policy towards determining the evaluation of ADJUNCT instructors, Broken Out by Public or Private Institutional Status 75

Table 5.12: Description of college's policy towards determining the evaluation of ADJUNCT instructors, Broken Out by Full Time Equivalent Enrollment 76

Table 5.13: Percentage of colleges that commonly use student evaluation forms to evaluate adjunct instructors 76

Table 5.14: Percentage of colleges that commonly use student evaluation forms to evaluate adjunct instructors, Broken Out by Type of College 76

Table 5.15: Percentage of colleges that commonly use student evaluation forms to evaluate adjunct instructors, Broken Out by Public or Private Institutional Status 76

Table 5.16: Percentage of colleges that commonly use student evaluation forms to evaluate adjunct instructors, Broken Out by Full Time Equivalent Enrollment 77

Table 5.17: Percentage of colleges that commonly use standardized tests to evaluate adjunct instructors 77

Table 5.18: Percentage of colleges that commonly use standardized tests to evaluate adjunct instructors, Broken Out by Type of College 77

Table 5.19: Percentage of colleges that commonly use standardized tests to evaluate adjunct instructors, Broken Out by Public or Private Institutional Status 77

Table 5.20: Percentage of colleges that commonly use standardized tests to evaluate adjunct instructors, Broken Out by Full Time Equivalent Enrollment 77

Table 5.21: Percentage of colleges that commonly use in class visits by full-time professors to evaluate adjunct instructors 78

Table 5.22: Percentage of colleges that commonly use in class visits by full-time professors to evaluate adjunct instructors, Broken Out by Type of College 78

Table 5.23: Percentage of colleges that commonly use in class visits by full-time professors to evaluate adjunct instructors, Broken Out by Public or Private Institutional Status   78

Table 5.24: Percentage of colleges that commonly use in class visits by full-time professors to evaluate adjunct instructors, Broken Out by Full Time Equivalent Enrollment   78

Table 5.25: Percentage of colleges that commonly use student evaluation forms to evaluate instructors 78

Table 5.26: Percentage of colleges that commonly use student evaluation forms to evaluate instructors, Broken Out by Type of College 79

Table 5.27: Percentage of colleges that commonly use student evaluation forms to evaluate instructors, Broken Out by Public or Private Institutional Status 79

Table 5.28: Percentage of colleges that commonly use student evaluation forms to evaluate instructors, Broken Out by Full Time Equivalent Enrollment 79

Table 5.29: Percentage of colleges that commonly use standardized tests to evaluate student learning in chosen majors 79

Table 5.30: Percentage of colleges that commonly use standardized tests to evaluate student learning in chosen majors, Broken Out by Type of College 79

Table 5.31: Percentage of colleges that commonly use standardized tests to evaluate student learning in chosen majors, Broken Out by Public or Private Institutional Status 80

Table 5.32: Percentage of colleges that commonly use standardized tests to evaluate student learning in chosen majors, Broken Out by Full Time Equivalent Enrollment 80

Table 5.33: Percentage of colleges that commonly use standardized tests provided by testing companies to obtain results to compare to national data 80
Table 5.34: Percentage of colleges that commonly use standardized tests provided by testing companies to obtain results to compare to national data to evaluate instructors, Broken Out by Type of College 80
Table 5.35: Percentage of colleges that commonly use standardized tests provided by testing companies to obtain results to compare to national data, Broken Out by Public or Private Institutional Status 80
Table 5.36: Percentage of colleges that commonly use standardized tests Provided by Testing Companies to Obtain Results to Compare to National Data to evaluate instructors, Broken Out by Full Time Equivalent Enrollment 81
Table 5.37: Percentage of colleges that commonly use In Class Visits by Full time professors or instructors or other evaluators to evaluate instructors 81
Table 5.38: Percentage of colleges that commonly use In Class Visits by Full time professors or instructors or other evaluators to evaluate instructors, Broken Out by Type of College   81
Table 5.39: Percentage of colleges that commonly use In Class Visits by Full time professors or instructors or other evaluators to evaluate instructors, Broken Out by Public or Private Institutional Status 81
Table 5.40: Percentage of colleges that commonly use In Class Visits by Full time professors or instructors or other evaluators to evaluate instructors, Broken Out by Full Time Equivalent Enrollment 81
Table 6.1: Description of college faculty's role in developing the college's assessment vehicles   82
Table 6.2: Description of college faculty's role in developing the college's assessment vehicles, Broken Out by Type of College 82
Table 6.3: Description of college faculty's role in developing the college's assessment vehicles, Broken Out by Public or Private Institutional Status 82
Table 6.4: Description of college faculty's role in developing the college's assessment vehicles, Broken Out by Full Time Equivalent Enrollment 83
Table 6.5: Description of college faculty's views of the assessment efforts of the college administration 83
Table 6.6: Description of college faculty's views of the assessment efforts of the college administration, Broken Out by Type of College 83
Table 6.7: Description of college faculty's views of the assessment efforts of the college administration, Broken Out by Public or Private Institutional Status 84
Table 6.8: Description of college faculty's views of the assessment efforts of the college administration, Broken Out by Full Time Equivalent Enrollment 84
Table 6.9: Percentage of colleges in the sample that have one or more centers to develop faculty teaching skills 84
Table 6.10: Percentage of colleges in the sample that have one or more centers to develop faculty teaching skills, Broken Out by Type of College 84
Table 6.11: Percentage of colleges in the sample that have one or more centers to develop faculty teaching skills, Broken Out by Public or Private Institutional Status 85
Table 6.12: Percentage of colleges in the sample that have one or more centers to develop faculty teaching skills, Broken Out by Full Time Equivalent Enrollment 85

Survey of Assessment Practices in Higher Education

Table 6.13: Mean, Median, Minimum and Maximum approximate annual spending for staff, office space, software, and other costs for colleges in the sample that have such centers (In $ US) 85

Table 6.14: Mean, Median, Minimum and Maximum annual spending for staff, office space, software, and other costs for colleges in the sample that have such centers, Broken Out by Type of College (In $ US) 85

Table 6.15: Mean, Median, Minimum and Maximum annual spending for staff, office space, software, and other costs for colleges in the sample that have such centers, Broken Out by Public or Private Institutional Status (In $ US) 86

Table 6.16: Mean, Median, Minimum and Maximum annual spending for staff, office space, software, and other costs for colleges in the sample that have such centers, Broken Out by Full Time Equivalent Enrollment (In $ US) 86

Table 6.17: Percentages of colleges in the sample that say they have a clear policy to link instructor compensation to documented increases in teaching effectiveness 86

Table 6.18: Percentages of colleges in the sample that say they have a clear policy to link instructor compensation to documented increases in teaching effectiveness, Broken Out by Type of College 86

Table 6.19: Percentages of colleges in the sample that say they have a clear policy to link instructor compensation to documented increases in teaching effectiveness, Broken Out by Public or Private Institutional Status 87

Table 6.20: Percentages of colleges in the sample that say they have a clear policy to link instructor compensation to documented increases in teaching effectiveness, Broken Out by Full Time Equivalent Enrollment 87

Table 7.1: Percentage of colleges that have a tutoring or student learning center 88

Table 7.2: Percentage of colleges that have a tutoring or student learning center, Broken Out by Type of College 88

Table 7.3: Percentage of colleges that have a tutoring or student learning center, Broken Out by Public or Private Institutional Status 88

Table 7.4: Percentage of colleges that have a tutoring or student learning center, Broken Out by Full Time Equivalent Enrollment 88

Table 7.5: Description of the location of the tutoring or learning center for colleges that have one 88

Table 7.6: Description of the location of the tutoring or learning center for colleges that have one, Broken Out by Type of College 89

Table 7.7: Description of the location of the tutoring or learning center for colleges that have one, Broken Out by Public or Private institutional status 89

Table 7.8: Description of the location of the tutoring or learning center for colleges that have one, Broken Out by Full time Equivalent Enrollment 89

Table 8.1: Percentage of colleges that survey student satisfaction with student services such as the food service, dormitory services, bookstore, library, etc. 90

Table 8.2: Percentage of colleges that survey student satisfaction with student services such as the food service, dormitory services, bookstore, library, etc. , Broken Out by Type of College 90

Table 8.3: Percentage of colleges that survey student satisfaction with student services such as the food service, dormitory services, bookstore, library, etc. , Broken Out by Public or Private Institutional Status 90

Survey of Assessment Practices in Higher Education

Table 8.4:   Percentage of colleges that survey student satisfaction with student services such as the food service, dormitory services, bookstore, library, etc. , Broken Out by Full Time Equivalent Enrollment 90

Table 9.1:   Percentage of colleges sampled that offer an annual "assessment day" or "assessment workshop" or "assessment seminar" or its equivalent for faculty and staff. 91

Table 9.2:   Percentage of colleges sampled that offer an annual "assessment day" or "assessment workshop" or "assessment seminar" or its equivalent for faculty and staff, Broken Out by Type of College 91

Table 9.3:   Percentage of colleges sampled that offer an annual "assessment day" or "assessment workshop" or "assessment seminar" or its equivalent for faculty and staff, Broken Out by Public or Private Institutional Status 91

Table 9.4:   Percentage of colleges sampled that offer an annual "assessment day" or "assessment workshop" or "assessment seminar" or its equivalent for faculty and staff, Broken Out by Full Time Equivalent Enrollment 91

Table 10.1:   Description of the success of assessment efforts for colleges sampled 92

Table 10.2:   Description of the success of assessment efforts for colleges sampled, Broken Out by Type of College 92

Table 10.3:   Description of the success of assessment efforts for colleges sampled, Broken Out by Public or Private Institutional Status 92

Table 10.4:   Description of the success of assessment efforts for colleges sampled, Broken Out by Full Time Equivalent Enrollment 93

Table 11.1:   Percentage of colleges sampled that have ever purchased student performance benchmarking data to compare their students' performance to that of national norms 94

Table 11.2:   Percentage of colleges sampled that have ever purchased student performance benchmarking data to compare their students' performance to that of national norms, Broken Out by Type of College 94

Table 11.3:   Percentage of colleges sampled that have ever purchased student performance benchmarking data to compare their students' performance to that of national norms, Broken Out by Public or Private Institutional Status 94

Table 11.4:   Percentage of colleges sampled that have ever purchased student performance benchmarking data to compare their students' performance to that of national norms, Broken Out by Full Time Equivalent Enrollment 94

Table 11.5:   Percentage of colleges sampled that use ZOOMERANG for assessment purposes   94

Table 11.6:   Percentage of colleges sampled that use ZOOMERANG for assessment purposes, Broken Out by Type of College 95

Table 11.7:   Percentage of colleges sampled that use ZOOMERANG for assessment purposes, Broken Out by Public or Private Institutional Status 95

Table 11.8:   Percentage of colleges sampled that use ZOOMERANG for assessment purposes, Broken Out by Full Time Equivalent Enrollment 95

Table 11.9:   Percentage of colleges sampled that use WEAVEONLINE for assessment purposes   95

Table 11.10:   Percentage of colleges sampled that use WEAVEONLINE for assessment purposes, Broken Out by Type of College 95

Table 11.11: Percentage of colleges sampled that use WEAVEONLINE for assessment purposes, Broken Out by Public or Private Institutional Status 96
Table 11.12: Percentage of colleges sampled that use WEAVEONLINE for assessment purposes, Broken Out by Full Time Equivalent Enrollment 96
Table 11.13: Percentage of colleges sampled that use SURVEYMONKEY for assessment purposes 96
Table 11.14: Percentage of colleges sampled that use SURVEYMONKEY for assessment purposes, Broken Out by Type of College 96
Table 11.15: Percentage of colleges sampled that use SURVEYMONKEY for assessment purposes, Broken Out by Public or Private Institutional Status 96
Table 11.16: Percentage of colleges sampled that use SURVEYMONKEY for assessment purposes, Broken Out by Full Time Equivalent Enrollment 97
Table 11.17: Percentage of colleges sampled that use WEBSURVEYOR for assessment purposes 97
Table 11.18: Percentage of colleges sampled that use WEBSURVEYOR for assessment purposes, Broken Out by Type of College 97
Table 11.19: Percentage of colleges sampled that use WEBSURVEYOR for assessment purposes, Broken Out by Public or Private Institutional Status 97
Table 11.20: Percentage of colleges sampled that use WEBSURVEYOR for assessment purposes, Broken Out by Full Time Equivalent Enrollment 97
Table 11.21: Percentage of colleges sampled that use STUDENTVOICE for assessment purposes 98
Table 11.22: Percentage of colleges sampled that use STUDENTVOICE for assessment purposes, Broken Out by Type of College 98
Table 11.23: Percentage of colleges sampled that use STUDENTVOICE for assessment purposes, Broken Out by Public or Private Institutional Status 98
Table 11.24: Percentage of colleges sampled that use STUDENTVOICE for assessment purposes, Broken Out by Full Time Equivalent Enrollment 98
Table 11.25: Percentage of colleges sampled that use KEY SURVEY for assessment purposes 98
Table 11.26: Percentage of colleges sampled that use KEY SURVEY for assessment purposes, Broken Out by Type of College 99
Table 11.27: Percentage of colleges sampled that use KEY SURVEY for assessment purposes, Broken Out by Public or Private Institutional Status 99
Table 11.28: Percentage of colleges sampled that use KEY SURVEY for assessment purposes, Broken Out by Full Time Equivalent Enrollment 99
Table 11.29: Percentage of colleges sampled that use SURVEY TRACKER PLUS for assessment purposes 99
Table 11.30: Percentage of colleges sampled that use SURVEY TRACKER PLUS for assessment purposes, Broken Out by Type of College 99
Table 11.31: Percentage of colleges sampled that use SURVEY TRACKER PLUS for assessment purposes, Broken Out by Public or Private Institutional Status 100
Table 11.32: Percentage of colleges sampled that use SURVEY TRACKER PLUS for assessment purposes, Broken Out by Full Time Equivalent Enrollment 100
Table 11.33: Percentage of colleges sampled that use SNAP for assessment purposes 100

Table 11.34: Percentage of colleges sampled that use SNAP for assessment purposes, Broken Out by Type of College 100
Table 11.35: Percentage of colleges sampled that use SNAP for assessment purposes, Broken Out by Public or Private Institutional Status 100
Table 11.36: Percentage of colleges sampled that use SNAP for assessment purposes, Broken Out by Full Time Equivalent Enrollment 101
Table 11.37: Percentage of colleges sampled that use FLASHLIGHT ONLINE for assessment purposes 101
Table 11.38: Percentage of colleges sampled that use FLASHLIGHT ONLINE for assessment purposes, Broken Out by Type of College 101
Table 11.39: Percentage of colleges sampled that use FLASHLIGHT ONLINE for assessment purposes, Broken Out by Public or Private Institutional Status 101
Table 11.40: Percentage of colleges sampled that use FLASHLIGHT ONLINE for assessment purposes, Broken Out by Full Time Equivalent Enrollment 101
Table 11.41: Percentage of colleges sampled that use ULTIMATE SURVEY for assessment purposes 102
Table 11.42: Percentage of colleges sampled that use ULTIMATE SURVEY for assessment purposes, Broken Out by Type of College 102
Table 11.43: Percentage of colleges sampled that use ULTIMATE SURVEY for assessment purposes, Broken Out by Public or Private Institutional Status 102
Table 11.44: Percentage of colleges sampled that use ULTIMATE SURVEY for assessment purposes, Broken Out by Full Time Equivalent Enrollment 102
Table 12.1: Mean, Median, Minimum and Maximum spending by the college administration on outside consultants, reports, conferences and other consulting services related to assessment within the past year (in $U.S.) 103
Table 12.2: Mean, Median, Minimum and Maximum spending by the college administration on outside consultants, reports, conferences and other consulting services related to assessment within the past year, Broken Out by Type of College (in $U.S.). 103
Table 12.3: Mean, Median, Minimum and Maximum spending by the college administration on outside consultants, reports, conferences and other consulting services related to assessment within the past year, Broken Out by Public or Private Institutional Status (in $U.S.) 103
Table 12.4: Mean, Median, Minimum and Maximum spending by the college administration on outside consultants, reports, conferences and other consulting services related to assessment within the past year, Broken Out by Full Time Equivalent Enrollment (in $U.S.) 104
Table 12.5: Mean, Median, Minimum and Maximum approximate number of conferences devoted to assessment issues that ADMINISTRATORS from colleges surveyed attended in the past year 104
Table 12.6: Mean, Median, Minimum and Maximum approximate number of conferences devoted to assessment issues that ADMINISTRATORS from colleges surveyed attended in the past year, Broken Out by Type of College 104
Table 12.7: Mean, Median, Minimum and Maximum approximate number of conferences devoted to assessment issues that ADMINISTRATORS from colleges surveyed attended in the past year, Broken Out by Public or Private Institutional Status 104

Table 12.8: Mean, Median, Minimum and Maximum approximate number of conferences devoted to assessment issues that ADMINISTRATORS from colleges surveyed attended in the past year, Broken Out by Full Time Equivalent Enrollment .. 105

Table 13.1: Percentage of colleges surveyed that have a post graduate assessment program 106

Table 13.2: Percentage of colleges surveyed that have a post graduate assessment program, Broken Out by Type of College... 106

Table 13.3: Percentage of colleges surveyed that have a post graduate assessment program, Broken Out by Public or Private Institutional Status...................................... 106

Table 13.4: Percentage of colleges surveyed that have a post graduate assessment program, Broken Out by Full Time Equivalent Enrollment 106

Table 13.5: Percentage of colleges surveyed that at least once per year conduct INTERVIEWS OF STUDENTS WHO GRADUATE 106

Table 13.6: Percentage of colleges surveyed that conduct at least once per year INTERVIEWS OF STUDENTS WHO GRADUATE, Broken Out by Type of College 107

Table 13.7: Percentage of colleges surveyed that conduct at least once per year INTERVIEWS OF STUDENTS WHO GRADUATE, Broken Out By Public or Private Institutional Status... 107

Table 13.8: Percentage of colleges surveyed that conduct INTERVIEWS OF STUDENTS WHO GRADUATE at least once per year, Broken Out by Full Time Equivalent Enrollment.. 107

Table 13.9: Percentage of colleges surveyed that conduct at least once per year INTERVIEWS OF STUDENTS WHO TRANSFER OUT OF COLLEGE 107

Table 13.10: Percentage of colleges surveyed that conduct at least once per year INTERVIEWS OF STUDENTS WHO TRANSFER OUT OF COLLEGE, Broken Out by Type of College... 108

Table 13.11: Percentage of colleges surveyed that conduct at least once per year INTERVIEWS OF STUDENTS WHO TRANSFER OUT OF COLLEGE, Broken Out by Public or Private Institutional Status.. 108

Table 13.12: Percentage of colleges surveyed that conduct at least once per year INTERVIEWS OF STUDENTS WHO TRANSFER OUT OF COLLEGE, Broken Out by Full Time Equivalent Enrollment... 108

Table 13.13: Percentage of colleges surveyed that conduct at least once per year INTERVIEWS OF STUDENTS WHO DROP OUT OF COLLEGE 108

Table 13.14: Percentage of colleges surveyed that conduct at least once per year INTERVIEWS OF STUDENTS WHO DROP OUT OF THE COLLEGE, Broken Out by Type of College 109

Table 13.15: Percentage of colleges surveyed that conduct at least once per year INTERVIEWS OF STUDENTS WHO DROP OUT OF THE COLLEGE, Broken Out by Public or Private Institutional Status.. 109

Table 13.16: Percentage of colleges surveyed that conduct at least once per year INTERVIEWS OF STUDENTS WHO DROP OUT OF THE COLLEGE, Broken Out by Full Time Equivalent Enrollment... 109

Table 13.17: Mean, Median, Minimum and Maximum approximate number of exit interviews conducted with graduating students 109

Table 13.18: Mean, Median, Minimum and Maximum approximate number of exit interviews conducted with graduating students, Broken Out by Type of College.......... 110

Table 13.19: Mean, Median, Minimum and Maximum approximate number of exit interviews conducted with graduating students, Broken Out by Public or Private Institutional Status.. 110

Table 13.20: Mean, Median, Minimum and Maximum approximate number of exit interviews conducted with graduating students, Broken Out by Full Time Equivalent Enrollment   110

Table 13.21: Mean, Median, Minimum and Maximum approximate number of exit interviews conducted with students who left the college for any reason in the past year   110

Table 13.22: Mean, Median, Minimum and Maximum approximate number of exit interviews conducted with students who left the college for any reason in the past year, Broken Out by Public or Private Institutional Status 111

Table 13.23: Mean, Median, Minimum and Maximum approximate number of exit interviews conducted with students who left the college for any reason in the past year, Broken Out by Full Time Equivalent Enrollment... 111

Table 13.24: Percentage of colleges that offer compensation of any kind for students that take exit interviews.. 111

Table 13.25: Percentage of colleges that offer compensation of any kind for students that take exit interviews, Broken Out by Type of College... 111

Table 13.26: Percentage of colleges that offer compensation of any kind for students that take exit interviews, Broken Out by Public or Private Institutional Status............... 111

Table 13.27: Percentage of colleges that offer compensation of any kind for students that take exit interviews, Broken Out by Full Time Equivalent Enrollment................... 112

Survey of Assessment Practices in Higher Education

College Demographic Information

Eighty three colleges participated in the survey and the tables below relate the distribution of survey participants by type and size

Type of College

	Community College	Primarily a 4-year Degree Granting Institution	An MA or PHD Granting Institution	Research University
Entire Sample	15.48%	40.48%	25.00%	19.05%

Public or Private Institutional Status

	Public Institution	Private Institution
Entire Sample	64.29%	35.71%

Summary of Main Findings

Summary Chapter 1: Departmental Assessment

Developing an Assessment Plan

Two thirds of the colleges in the sample say that they require academic departments to develop an assessment plan identifying key concepts and ideas that students should master. Only 3.57% say that they do not require this, and close to 30% say that though they don't require it, they are working on it.

Community colleges and research universities were the most likely to have this requirement, and more public than private colleges had this key requirement. College size did not appear to have any impact on the tendency to require academic departments to develop an assessment plan.

Assessment Plan

A mean of close to 70% of the academic departments in the colleges in the sample have developed detailed assessment plans, though the range is quite broad, from none to all. The smallest colleges, those with 2,500 or fewer students, tended to lag behind the others.

Assessment Office

38.1% of the colleges in the sample have an assessment office (or its functional equivalent) that communicate with all or most academic departments through a designated assessment coordinator; 13.1% communicate only to some departments this way, and a little less than half, 48.81%, do not have such designated coordinators for any academic departments.

Use of Software to Aid in Assessment

Community colleges were more likely to use software packages to aid in assessment, making up the majority of users for each package in the survey.

Concerning the use of specific software packages for assessment, only 4.7% say they use the ACT; all users were public community colleges. No other colleges polled use ACT.

16.7% of colleges sampled say they use the Accuplacer Assessment Package; a majority of those (61.5%) were community colleges.

The COMPASS Assessment Package was the most popular overall, with 19.05% of schools polled saying they use it. Its use among public and private schools was comparable; 20.37% and 16.67% respectively. It was also the package whose use was most evenly distributed among varying enrollment levels of schools, only dropping to 13.6% usage in the highest category (15,000+ FTE). No research universities polled used the COMPASS.

The writing section of COMPASS was the least often administered part of package to incoming freshmen; 15.5% of the sample used the COMPASS Writing test. Public colleges were more likely to administer it than were private colleges. The mathematics and reading sections were more likely to be used in general, with each being used by close to 20% of colleges polled.

Other assessment tools, including the NSSE, HERI, Educational Benchmarking, Inc., the Center for Educational Assessment, and Chalk and Wire EPortfolio were more likely to be used by private colleges. The Center for Education Assessment, and Chalk and Wire EPortfolio were used by 3.57%, and 4.76% respectively of the colleges in the sample.

By far the most popular tool was the NSSE, used by nearly 61% of colleges sampled, followed by the HERI and Educational Benchmarking Inc., at use levels of 33.33%, and 23.81% respectively.

Summary Chapter 2: Standardized Testing

Remedial Courses

Remedial or developmental courses were more likely to be offered at small colleges and community colleges. 100% of community colleges polled offered such courses in writing, and mathematics. 69% offered courses in study skills, and nearly 77% offered remedial courses in English as a Second Language. Between 50% and 71% of other colleges offered remedial courses in writing and mathematics. Even 25% of research universities in the sample offered remedial skills classes.

Among non-community colleges offering developmental courses in English as a Second Language, MA/PHD granting schools most frequently offered this option, with nearly 43% offering such courses. About one quarter of 4-year colleges, and research universities polled offered them.

Only 4.76% of the colleges in the sample offered remedial courses in information or computer literacy; these were offered only by community colleges and BA-degree granting colleges in the sample.

Payout for Standardized Testing

Most colleges do not pay students to take standardized tests that are used internally for assessment purposes but among those that do, public colleges spent more than private college. Public colleges spent a mean of $2711.67; private colleges, a mean of $362.50.

Research universities spent, on average, considerably more than any other type of school, a mean of $8333.33 and a maximum of $20,000. 4-Year colleges spent a mean of only $1194.41, with a maximum of $10,000.

Also, spending rose with enrollment. There was a steady rise in both the mean and the maximum spending across the four FTE groups (Table 2.24).

For the entire sample, only 1.23% offer a higher rate of pay to students that score higher on standardized assessment tests used internally by the college, on the theory that this encourages full student effort. One public research university with a FTE of between 6,000 and 15,000 students accounted for all colleges in the sample with this policy.

Summary Chapter 3: Assessment Office

Percentage of Colleges with an Assessment Office

More than 50% of colleges in the sample said that they have an office of assessment, or similar department that primarily devotes itself to assessment. Another 38% said that they instead have an official in charge of assessment that works for another academic office or department. Only 9.5% of colleges in the sample said that they do not have an assessment official.

The tendency to have an "assessment guru" or "assessment dean" or other such type did not differ much among the various college types. 46.15% of community colleges have a chief assessment official while close to 56% of BA-granting institutions did, and this was the ceiling and floor in the data among the college types. Public colleges (57.41%) were more likely to have an assessment czar than were private colleges, (43.33%). Almost two thirds of the colleges with 15,000 or more students FTE have a chief assessment official of some kind.

Full Time Assessment Employees

The mean number of full-time employees for the office of assessment was 1.9, with a median of 1. Research universities had the largest assessment offices, averaging 3.1 employees.

The maximum number of such employees for research universities in the sample was 13, followed by 12 for MA/PHD Schools, 3 for 4-Year Schools, and 1.5 for community colleges.

Public colleges hired more than twice as many full-time assessment employees than did the private colleges (a mean of 2.49 and 1.06 respectively). As the size of the college increased, so did the mean, median, minimum and maximum number of assessment office employees, with the biggest jump coming between schools with a FTE of between

6,000 and 15,000 students and colleges with more than 15,000 students, which had respective means of 1.68 and 3.78 assessment office employees.

Assessment Office Salary Range

Close to half of the chief assessment officers in the sample earned salaries of between $61,000 and $99,000 while close to 19% earned more than $99,000 and about 34% earned less than $61,000.

The average salary range was generally higher among MA/PHD schools and research universities; private colleges generally gave lower salaries than public colleges. Only 5.56% of those polled said that their highest ranking assessment official made more than $99,000 while a third earned less than $50,000.

All chief assessment officials earning less than $50,000 annually worked for colleges with less than 6,000 students, FTE.

Assessment Office Size

The mean size of the assessment offices in the sample was 691 square feet with a median of just 200 square feet.

The size of the assessment office for colleges in the sample varied most between public and private institutions. Private institutions had offices with a mean size of 170.33 square feet; the mean was 1059.00 square feet for public colleges. Office size increased with size of FTE enrollment, increasing from a mean of only 162.4 square feet for colleges with less than 2,500 students FTE, to 1,870 square feet for colleges with 15,000 or more students FTE.

Annual Assessment Office Budget

The mean annual budget, including salaries and overhead, of the assessment offices in the sample was $195,069. MA/PHD schools had significantly higher budgets overall, with a mean of $749,000 and a maximum budget of $1,400,000, followed by research universities with a mean of $234,000 and a maximum of $402,000. The mean assessment office budget for public colleges was more than twice that of private colleges ($245,523 to $101,370), and the minimum for a private college was just $14,000. For public colleges the minimum was $40,000.

As enrollment increased, so did assessment office budgets.

Assessment Professionals Working Outside of the Main Assessment Office

The mean number of assessment professionals working in other offices outside of the main college assessment office was 3.1. Community colleges had the highest mean, 5.72.

This figure represents professionals who perform assessment duties in addition to their normal faculty duties. For 4-year schools, MA/PHD schools, and research universities these numbers are much lower – ranging from 1.5 to 3.22.

Public colleges were far more likely than private colleges to have assessment professionals working outside of the assessment office. The mean number of assessment professionals working outside of the college assessment office for public colleges was 4.52, the median 2, and the maximum 35. Private colleges, by comparison, had almost none, with a mean of 0.77, a median of 0, and a maximum of 5. The largest colleges, those with a FTE of 15,000 or more students, had the highest mean and maximum number of professionals working outside the assessment office (8.43, and 35 respectively).

Size of the Basic Instructor Evaluation Form

For the entire sample, the mean and median number of questions on the basic instructor evaluation form given to students was almost identical, at 20.62 and 20.0 respectively. The range was from two questions to sixty five!

Community colleges, 4-Year schools, and MA/PHD schools each had questionnaires averaging 21 questions. Research universities were the only type of institution with a significantly different mean, 16 questions. Research universities also had the lowest minimum and maximum number of questions.

The difference between the number of questions on the evaluation form for public and private colleges was negligible. Again, the FTE of the college had little effect on the size of the evaluation form. All figures were comparable across all FTE categories.

Summary Chapter 4: Student Assessment of Instructors

Questionnaires

All colleges in the sample used questionnaires for student assessment of instructors, and only 2.38% said that such questionnaires were used for only for a small percentage of faculty.

30.95% said that questionnaires were used to evaluate most faculty, with some exceptions, and roughly two thirds of the entire sample said that all faculty were assessed through questionnaires.

Community colleges were the least likely to use questionnaire assessment for all faculty, with only 53% saying that this was the case. Research universities were the most likely to evaluate faculty with student questionnaires; 81.25% used questionnaires to evaluate all faculty, and none reported no use of these questionnaires at all, or use for a small percentage of faculty.

One third of MA/PHD schools use questionnaires for most faculty, and the remaining two thirds use them for all faculty. Similarly, two thirds of public colleges used questionnaires for all faculty, and 29.63% used them for most faculty.

100% of colleges in the two largest enrollment categories use questionnaire assessment for most or all faculty.

Impact of Student Assessment Questionnaires on Tenure Decisions.

8.64% of the colleges in the entire sample said that student faculty questionnaires had no impact on tenure decisions while 26% said that they had significant impact. Another 14.81% said they had slight impact and a shade more than half said that they "have some impact." Interestingly, surprisingly, and – we wonder – if entirely frankly – it was the research universities in the sample that said that student evaluations of instructors most frequently had a significant impact on tenure decisions. It was the community colleges that most often said that they had no impact, or only a slight impact on tenure decisions – results quite opposite of what we would have expected.

Roughly half of the colleges in the entire sample said that questionnaires have some impact on tenure decisions, and a little over a quarter said that they have a significant impact.

MA/PHD schools seemed to be the most unanimous, with 65% saying that questionnaires have some impact, and 25% saying that they have a significant impact. The remaining 10% said that questionnaires have a slight impact, and none said that they had no impact at all.

Public and private college demographics were comparable. Colleges in the highest two FTE categories were more likely to consider student evaluation of faculty questionnaires for tenure decisions, at least ostensibly. Roughly 80% of each said that these student evaluations had some or a significant impact on tenure decisions.

Impact of Student Faculty Assessment Questionnaires on the Hiring and Retention of Adjunct Instructors

Overall, about three quarters of those colleges surveyed said that student evaluation of faculty through questionnaires had some or a significant impact on hiring, advancement and retention decisions regarding adjuncts.

For the entire sample, the differences between the impact of faculty assessment questionnaires on the hiring and retention of adjunct instructors was nearly identical to the impact the same surveys have on tenure decisions for other faculty.

However, when broken out for type of college the numbers become more varied.

One quarter of community colleges said that the questionnaires had a significant impact on the retention of adjunct instructors, compared to just 16.67% for tenure decisions. 4-Year and MA/PHD Schools had comparable numbers regarding both, but for research universities evaluation questionnaires meant more for the hiring and retention of adjunct faculty than for tenure decisions for regular faculty. 87.5% of the research universities said that questionnaires had some or a significant impact on the retention of adjunct instructors, compared to 75% for the impact on tenure decisions.

Far more private colleges used the questionnaire data for adjunct faculty retention decisions than for tenure decisions.

Smaller colleges in the sample were divided on the use of assessment questionnaires for retention decisions for adjunct faculty. 37.5% of colleges with a FTE of 2,500 or less said that such questionnaires have some impact, 29.17% said they have a significant impact, and 16.67% said they have a slight impact. The remaining 16.67% said that questionnaires have no impact at all.

Colleges in the larger FTE categories were less divided. More than 86% of those with an FTE of 15,000 or more said that instructor evaluation questionnaires given to students have some or a significant impact on retention and other personnel decisions relating to adjunct instructors.

Formats Used for the Completion of Student Assessment Questionnaires

The majority (61.90%) of the colleges in the entire sample exclusively used a paper format for the completion of assessment questionnaires.

More than 60% of community colleges, 4-Year colleges, and MA/PHD colleges in the sample exclusively use a paper format; 43.75% of research universities only use the paper format.

Nearly a quarter (23.53%) of 4-year colleges offered either online or paper formats. For MA/PHD Schools the number was similar (28.57%) Only 15.38% of community colleges offered both an online and paper format, but 43.75% of research universities offered both. On the whole, research universities were the most tech savvy, with a combined 56.25% of them offering an online student assessment survey option.

The public/private split was more uneven, especially for private colleges. More than half of public colleges sampled only use paper for their assessment questionnaires, and a third used both. 76.67% of private colleges use only the paper format and only 6.67% exclusively use online surveys.

Smaller colleges were primarily completely paper based, while colleges in the largest FTE category were mostly computer based. Mid-sized colleges tended mostly to use paper formats, but very few strictly used computer-based survey techniques. 11.11% of colleges with an FTE of between 2,500 and 6,000, and 5.26% of colleges with an FTE of between 6,000 and 15,000 used only an online format.

Impact of Student Course Evaluations on Merit Pay Increases for Instructors

53.16% of colleges in the sample said that student course evaluations don't have much of an effect on merit pay increases for instructors, and 8.86% said that such evaluations are an important factor in merit pay decisions. The rest said that course evaluations are at least taken into account

All community colleges surveyed said that student instructor evaluations don't have an affect on merit pay increases. This percentage decreased significantly for 4-year colleges (56.25%), and then again for MA/PHD schools (36.84%). Research universities were the most likely to consider course evaluations in the evaluation of merit pay increases. 18.75 said that they are an important factor in such decisions. It may be somewhat perverse, but the reality seems to be the opposite of what some might expect. The more research oriented an institution, the more it seems to take into account student's opinions of instructors, or at least the more anxious they are to appear to be taking this into account.

The data for public and private colleges were fairly similar, and consistent with statistics for the entire sample. Public colleges were just as likely as private colleges to take student course evaluations into account, or not.

The largest schools, with a FTE of 15,000 or more students, were the most likely to consider course evaluations in merit pay decisions, with 50% saying that they are taken into account, and 13.64% saying that they are an important factor in merit pay decisions.

Summary Chapter 5: Evaluation of Adjunct Faculty

Courses Taught by Adjunct Faculty

Approximately 28.55% of courses for colleges in the entire sample are taught by adjunct faculty. The median was 25%, with a minimum of 5%, a maximum of 75%.

Community colleges had a much higher percentage of courses taught by adjunct faculty, 10% higher than the next highest mean of roughly 36% for MA/PHD Schools. Community colleges also had a much higher minimum (25% compared to 8% for the next highest minimum, again for MA/PHD schools). Adjunct faculty taught roughly a fifth of the courses offered by the 4-year colleges and research universities in the sample.

Adjuncts taught 19.38% of private college courses in the sample, compared to just over 35% for public colleges.

Adjunct faculty taught the highest percentage of total courses at midsize colleges.

Methods of Evaluating Adjunct Faculty

42.11% of the colleges in the entire sample said that the college administration determines the method for evaluating adjunct faculty; 47.37% said the decision is left up to individual departments. 10.53% said that they have no official policy on this.

More than half of community colleges and 4-Year schools had policies determined by the central college administration while just a bit more than 28% of research and MA/PHD granting institutions relied on the college administration to determine methods for the evaluation of adjunct faculty.

Private colleges were more likely to have their method determined by the administration; half of colleges sampled used this method, compared to 38% for public colleges. Roughly one fifth of private colleges, however, didn't have a policy or method for evaluating adjunct faculty. Only 6% of public colleges said they didn't have a method.

22.73% of the schools in the lowest FTE category didn't have an official policy, but this percentage dropped to 6.67% for schools in the next highest category. For the next to largest category this number was 10.53%, but no college in the highest category, those schools with a FTE of 15,000 or more students reported not having an official policy. 60% of schools in the highest FTE category said that evaluation was left up to individual academic departments.

Policy On Determining The Evaluation of Adjunct Faculty

For the entire sample, 32.05% said that determining the evaluation of adjunct faculty is left to each academic department, 20.51 percent said that the policy is determined by the college administration, and 37.18% said the decision is based on a mix of input from the departments and the administration. The remaining 10.26% didn't have a clear policy.

Fifty percent of community colleges, the highest percentage of all college types sampled, evaluated adjuncts through a mix of input from departments and the central administration. None of the research universities said that the policy is determined solely by the college administration. Instead, there was an even split with 42.86% saying their policy is determined by each department, and 42.86% saying that the policy is determined by the departments and the administration together. Private colleges were more likely to not have a clear policy, with 18.52% reporting this, compared to 5.88% for public colleges. Private colleges tended to have their policy determined by the administration, while public colleges favored the departments. Both types of schools had a high percentage reporting that their policy is determined by a mix of input, but the percentage for public colleges was much higher (43.14% to 25.93%).
Statistics for the two smallest FTE categories were comparable, with the main difference being between schools that determine their policy with a mix of input. For schools with a

FTE of 6,000 or more emphasis shifts to both the departments, and a mixed input policy, and for schools in the highest category (15,000+) only 5% said that their policy was determined by the administration. Half said that it was a mixed input, and the other 45% said that the departments determined the policy. Also, as the FTE increased the number of schools reporting a lack of policy decreased such that no schools in the highest category reported not having a policy.

The Evaluation of Adjunct Instructors

The Use of Student Evaluation Forms in Evaluating Adjunct Instructors

The overwhelming majority of colleges in the entire sample, nearly 92%, use some form of student evaluation form for the evaluation of adjunct faculty. Research universities used them the least, 87.5% used them, and MA/PHD Schools used them the most, 100% used the forms. There was little difference is use between public and private colleges.

Interestingly, colleges falling in the 2,501 to 6,000 FTE category were much less likely to use student evaluation forms. 77.78% used them, compared to 91.67% for the entire sample, and 90.91% for the next highest FTE category

The Use of Standardized Tests in Evaluating Adjunct Instructors

Only one college in the sample used standardized tests to evaluate adjunct instructors. This was a 4-Year, private college with an FTE of 2,500 or less.

The Use of In Class Visits by Full-Time Professors in Evaluating Adjunct Instructors

59.52% of the colleges in the sample use in class visits to evaluate adjunct instructors.

Half of 4-year colleges and research universities polled use this method, and roughly three quarters of community colleges and MA/PHD-level colleges.

A slightly higher percentage of private colleges than public colleges used in class visits to evaluate adjunct instructors. As the FTE of the college increased, the use of in class visits decreased. The drop, from 66.67% to 52.63%, occurred between schools with a FTE of between 2,500 and 6,000, and schools with a FTE of between 6,000 and 15,000.

Evaluating Instructors

The Use of Student Evaluation Forms in Evaluating Full Time Instructors

94.05% of colleges in the sample use student evaluation forms to evaluate full time instructors.

For type of college, the numbers do not deviate far from the entire sample, with the exception of MA/PHD schools. 100% of MA/PHD schools sampled said that they use student evaluation forms.

The FTE category reporting the lowest usage of student evaluation forms was the 2,501 to 6,000 FTE category, with 83.33%. The highest was the 6,001 to 14,999 category; all colleges in the category use student evaluation forms.

The Use of Standardized Tests to Evaluate Learning in Chosen Majors in Evaluating Instructors

Only 4.76% of the colleges sampled used standardized tests to evaluate performance in chosen academic majors. The greatest use came from MA/PHD school; the lowest by research universities, none of which use such tests. Nearly twice as many private than public colleges use standardized tests to evaluate learning in chosen majors, (6.67% to 3.7%). All use of tests to evaluate learning in chosen majors was by the smallest and largest colleges in terms of enrollment.

The Use of Standardized Tests Provided by Testing Companies to Obtain Results to Compare to National Data in Evaluating Instructors

Only 7.14% of colleges sampled use this type of standardized test. These are mostly private colleges, and all have a FTE of 6,000 or lese, the majority below 2,500 FTE. No research universities sampled use these tests.

The Use of In Class Visits by Full-Time Professors or Other Evaluators in Evaluating Instructors

The most common method of evaluating instructors was the use of in class visits; 65.48% of colleges sampled use them. Community colleges and MA/PHD-level schools used in-class visits the most (84.62% and 71.43% used them, respectively).

Public and private colleges used in-class visits to approximately the same degree; the difference in use among different sizes of schools was most apparent for the smallest schools. 72% of schools with a FTE of 2,500 or less used in-class visits methods, significantly higher than for the larger colleges.

Summary Chapter 6: Faculty Involvement in Assessment

Role of College Faculty in Developing the College's Assessment Vehicles

51.85% of colleges in the sample said that both the college administration and the faculty are intimately involved in developing the college's assessment vehicles. Only 6.17% said that it was largely an administration effort.

Community colleges were more likely to develop their assessment vehicles through dual input from administration and faculty, and research universities were the most likely to develop their vehicles with only some input from faculty.

Private colleges were more likely to either have dual input from faculty and staff. Public colleges were more likely to report that their efforts were primarily led by either the college administration, or primarily by faculty, but not both in unison.

On the whole, as the FTE of the school increased, the tendency to have a vehicle that is developed through dual input of faculty and administration increased. In the highest FTE category (15,000+ students) no schools reported developing their assessment vehicles through only an administration effort, and only 4.76% reported primarily a faculty developed assessment vehicle.

Faculty Views on Assessment Efforts

48% of the schools in the entire sample said that their faculty "pays lip service to the idea" of assessment but that they are not entirely enthused about it. This was the most common response.

Half of community colleges said that their faculty is on board with most initiatives, a much higher percentage than for other types of colleges. Community colleges also had the highest percentage distrustful of assessment. 20% in the sample were suspicious of assessment efforts, compared to the next highest, 15.38% for research universities.

Centers to Develop Faculty Teaching Skills

Slightly under two thirds of the colleges in the entire sample said that their college has one or more centers to develop faculty teaching skills. Research universities far surpassed the norm; 93.33% of those sampled have such a center. Public colleges were far more likely than private colleges to have one, and as the FTE increased, so did the likelihood of the school having a center.

Approximate Annual Assessment Office Spending

The mean annual spending for college assessment offices was $256,385, with research universities having a significantly higher mean of $850,000. Community colleges had the next highest mean. Private colleges spent significantly less than public colleges.

Policy to Link Instructor Compensation to Documented Increases in Teaching Effectiveness

Approximately 7.6% of the colleges in the sample say that they have a clear policy of linking instructor pay increases to documented increases in instructor effectiveness. Most colleges said that they do not have a policy. Those that do were primarily research universities, and schools with an FTE of 15,000 or more students.

Summary Chapter 7: Tutoring

Tutoring or Student Learning Center

About 94% of the colleges in the sample offer either tutoring or a student learning center. None of the few colleges that did not have a student learning center were 4-year degree granting schools, private colleges, or schools in the lowest FTE category. Community colleges were the least likely to offer a student learning center.

Location of the Tutoring or Learning Center

Colleges with a learning center tended to have a building devoted to it, except for 4-year colleges, half of which housed theirs in the library. Public colleges tended to have a devoted building, as well as roughly 89% of schools in the largest FTE Category.

Summary Chapter 8: Assessing Student Services

The majority of colleges in the sample did student satisfaction surveys. 4-year colleges, private colleges and small colleges were the least likely to do student satisfaction surveys. In fact, the larger the college, the more likely it was to do student satisfaction surveys. 95% of those in the largest FTE Category gave student satisfaction surveys.

Summary Chapter 9: Assessment Environment

30% of the colleges in the sample have an annual assessment day or its equivalent. These numbers were roughly consistent across the board for college type, public/private status, and FTE enrollment.

Summary Chapter 10: Curriculum Changes

Research universities most frequently had assessment offices, with the highest budgets, yet these universities among all survey participants found their assessment efforts most wanting. 26.67% reported that efforts had not led to any significant changes, and none of those in the sample said that they had led to dramatic changes. Community colleges seemingly gaining the most from assessment efforts, at least in their own eyes.

Summary Chapter 11: Use of Benchmarking Data

The Purchase of Student Performance Benchmarking Data

Nearly 44% of the colleges sampled have purchased student performance benchmarking data. More than half of the research universities and nearly half of the 4-year degree granting colleges have purchased student benchmarking data. More than 47% of public colleges use the data, while 37% of private colleges did so.

Colleges that use ZOOMERANG

16.67% of the colleges in the sample use the surveying application Zoomerang for assessment purposes; it was used mostly by community colleges and 4-year colleges. Only 6.25% of research universities used it.

Colleges that use WEAVEONLINE

4% of the colleges in the entire sample used WeaveOnline for assessment purposes; those using it were 4-year colleges and research universities.

Colleges that use SURVEYMONKEY

Nearly 37% of the colleges in the entire sample use SurveyMonkey for assessment purposes. SurveyMonkey was the most commonly used package. Nearly 41% of public colleges and 30% of private colleges used SurveyMonkey for assessment purposes. Use of SurveyMonkey for assessment purposes rose with the enrollment level of the college. Half of all colleges with 15,000 or more students FTE use SurveyMonkey for assessment purposes.

Colleges that use WEBSURVEYOR

9.52% of the colleges in the entire sample used this application for assessment purposes. These were all public colleges with FTE enrollments above 2,500 students.

Colleges that use STUDENTVOICE

2.4% of the colleges in the sample use STUDENTVOICE. All users were 4-year-level colleges.

Colleges that use KEY SURVEY

Only one college in the sample used this package for assessment purposes. This was a public community college, with an FTE of 15,000 or more students.

Colleges that use SURVEY TRACKER

2.38% of the colleges in the entire sample used Survey Tracker. These were all public community colleges with FTE Enrollments of 6,001 or more.

Colleges that use SNAP

Roughly 5% of the colleges in the sample used the application SNAP for assessment purposes.

Colleges that use FLASHLIGHT ONLINE

Roughly 6% of the colleges in the sample used the application Flashlight Online for assessment purposes. Flashlight Online was not used by any MA/PHD-level colleges in the sample.

Colleges that use ULTIMATE SURVEY

2.38% of the colleges in the entire sample used Ultimate Survey for assessment purposes. All users of this application were public 4-year colleges with FTE enrollments between 2,501 and 14,999 students.

Summary Chapter 12: Use of Consultants and Services

Spending on Outside Consultants and Services Related to Assessment

The colleges in the sample spent a mean of $12,984 on outside consultants, reports, conferences and other consulting services related to assessment. The range of spending was 0 to $75,000.

Community colleges spent the most by far on consultants related to assessment, a mean of more than $27,000; more than twice as much as the mean spending for the entire sample. Public colleges significantly outspent private colleges, and spending rose with enrollment size until the largest enrollment size group, in which colleges spent less than the norm.

Conferences Devoted to Assessment that Administrators Attended in the Past Year

The mean number of conferences on assessment issues attended by the assessment administrators in the sample in the past year was 2.58 with a median of 2.5. Public college assessment administrators attended close to 3 conferences per year while assessment administrators from the private colleges averaged close to 2 conferences.

Summary Chapter 13: Post Graduate Assessment

Colleges with a Post Graduate Assessment Program

About 37% of the colleges in the sample have a post graduate assessment program to ascertain how graduates perform in life after college. About 43% of research universities had post graduate assessment programs compared to only 25% of community colleges. Half of all colleges with enrollment of 15,000 or more have a post graduate assessment program.

Interviews of Students Who Graduate

Approximately 34.5% of the colleges in the sample conduct interviews of recent graduates at least once per year. 4-year degree granting colleges were the most likely to conduct such interviews, and more than 47% of these colleges in the sample conducted these interviews at least once per year. The smallest colleges, those with 2,500 or fewer students FTE, were the most likely to conduct interviews of recent graduates; 44% of these colleges conducted these interviews.

Interviews of Students Who Transfer Out of College

Research universities were the least likely to conduct interviews with students that transferred out of the college to another institution. Only 6.25% of the research universities in the sample did so compared to 35.29% for 4-year schools, and 23.53% for the entire sample. 40% of the colleges with 2,500 or fewer students regularly interviewed students who transferred out of the college.

Interviews of Students Who Drop Out of College

29.4% of the colleges in the sample conduct interviews at least once per year with students who drop out of the college. 4-year degree granting colleges were the most likely to conduct this kind of interview and research universities the least likely. Private colleges were nearly twice as likely as public colleges to conduct this kind of interview.

Number of Exit Interviews for Graduating Students

Colleges in the sample conducted a mean of 1,118 exit interviews with graduating students. Research universities conducted vastly more interviews than any other type of school, 3,381 mean interviews; the next highest was a mean of 938.5 interviews conducted by community colleges. The maximum for research universities was 10,000 yearly interviews, followed by 2,400 for 4-year colleges.

Exit Interviews Conducted With Students Who Left the College For Any Reason

Colleges in the sample conducted a mean of 129.3 interviews with students who had dropped out of the college in the past year for any reason.

Compensation for Students That Take Exit Interviews

3.7% of the colleges in the sample offer compensation for graduating or transferring students that take exit interviews; all of these were MA-PHD granting level colleges, and all were public colleges with between 2,500 and 15,000 students, FTE.

Chapter 1: Departmental Assessment

Table 1.1: Percentage of colleges in the sample that require that academic departments develop an assessment plan identifying key concepts and ideas that students should master

	Yes	No	No, but we are working on this
Entire Sample	66.67%	3.57%	29.76%

Table 1.2: Percentage of colleges in the sample that require that academic departments develop an assessment plan identifying key concepts and ideas that students should master, Broken Out by Type of College

Type of College	Yes	No	No, but we are working on this
Community College	76.92%	0.00%	23.08%
Primarily a 4-year Degree Granting Institution	66.67%	3.03%	30.30%
An MA or PHD Granting Institution	57.14%	4.76%	38.10%
Research University	75.00%	6.25%	18.75%

Table 1.3: Percentage of colleges in the sample that require that academic departments develop an assessment plan identifying key concepts and ideas that students should master, Broken Out by Public or Private Institutional Status

Public or Private Status	Yes	No	No, but we are working on this
Public College	71.70%	5.66%	22.64%
Private College	60.00%	0.00%	40.00%

Table 1.4: Percentage of colleges in the sample that require that academic departments develop an assessment plan identifying key concepts and ideas that students should master, Broken Out by Full time equivalent enrollment

Full Time Equivalent Enrollment	Yes	No	No, but we are working on this
2,500 or less	64.00%	4.00%	32.00%
2,501 to 6,000	72.22%	0.00%	27.78%
6,001 to 14,999	63.16%	10.53%	26.32%
15,000 or more	71.43%	0.00%	28.57%

Survey of Assessment Practices in Higher Education

Table 1.5: Mean, Median, Minimum and Maximum percentage of the major departments in the college that have developed a detailed assessment plan

	Mean	Median	Minimum	Maximum
Entire Sample	69.81	85.00	0.00	100.00

Table 1.6: Mean, Median, Minimum and Maximum percentage of the major departments in the college that have developed a detailed assessment plan, Broken Out by Type of College

Type of College	Mean	Median	Minimum	Maximum
Community College	65.73	85.00	0.00	98.00
Primarily a 4-year Degree Granting Institution	72.28	85.00	0.00	100.00
An MA or PHD Granting Institution	65.88	75.00	20.00	100.00
A Research University	72.50	92.50	0.00	100.00

Table 1.7: Mean, Median, Minimum and Maximum percentage of the major departments in the college that have developed a detailed assessment plan, Broken Out by Public or Private Institutional Status

Public or Private Status	Mean	Median	Minimum	Maximum
Public College	72.38	85.00	0.00	100.00
Private College	65.52	80.00	0.00	100.00

Table 1.8: Mean, Median, Minimum and Maximum percentage of the major departments in the college that have developed a detailed assessment plan, Broken Out by Full time equivalent enrollment

Full Time Equivalent Enrollment	Mean	Median	Minimum	Maximum
2,500 or less	58.92	72.50	0.00	100.00
2,501 to 6,000	77.13	90.00	0.00	100.00
6,001 to 14,999	72.00	80.00	20.00	100.00
15,000 or more	76.35	90.00	20.00	100.00

Survey of Assessment Practices in Higher Education

Table 1.9: Percentage of college assessment offices (or other office entrusted with this task) that communicate with academic departments through designated assessment coordinators in the various academic departments

	Yes, for all or most departments	Yes, for some departments	No, not really
Entire Sample	38.10%	13.10%	48.81%

Table 1.10: Percentage of college assessment offices (or other office entrusted with this task) that communicate with academic departments through designated assessment coordinators in the various academic departments, Broken Out by Type of College

Type of College	Yes, for all or most departments	Yes, for some departments	No, not really
Community College	30.77%	15.38%	53.85%
Primarily a 4-year Degree Granting Institution	47.06%	8.82%	44.12%
An MA or PHD Granting Institution	19.05%	23.81%	57.14%
A Research University	50.00%	6.25%	43.75%

Table 1.11: Percentage of college assessment offices (or other office entrusted with this task) that communicate with academic departments through designated assessment coordinators in the various academic departments, Broken Out by Public or Private Institutional Status

Public or Private Status	Yes, for all or most departments	Yes, for some departments	No, not really
Public College	37.04%	18.52%	44.44%
Private College	40.00%	3.33%	56.67%

Table 1.12: Percentage of college assessment offices (or other office entrusted with this task) that communicate with academic departments through designated assessment coordinators in the various academic departments, Broken Out by Full time equivalent enrollment

Full Time Equivalent Enrollment	Yes, for all or most departments	Yes, for some departments	No, not really
2,500 or less	44.00%	0.00%	56.00%
2,501 to 6,000	44.44%	16.67%	38.89%
6,001 to 14,999	21.05%	26.32%	52.63%
15,000 or more	40.91%	13.64%	45.45%

Survey of Assessment Practices in Higher Education

Table 1.13: Percentage of Colleges in the Sample that use the Assessment Package ACT

	Yes	No
Entire Sample	4.71%	94.12%

Table 1.14: Percentage of Colleges in the Sample that use the Assessment Package ACT, Broken Out by Type of College

Type of College	Yes	No
Community College	30.77%	69.23%
Primarily a 4-year Degree Granting Institution	0.00%	100.00%
An MA or PHD Granting Institution	0.00%	100.00%
A Research University	0.00%	100.00%

Table 1.15: Percentage of Colleges in the Sample that use the Assessment Package ACT, Broken Out by Public or Private Institutional Status

Public or Private Status	Yes	No
Public College	7.41%	92.59%
Private College	0.00%	100.00%

Table 1.16: Percentage of Colleges in the Sample that use the Assessment Package ACT, Broken Out by Full Time Equivalent Enrollment

Full Time Equivalent Enrollment	Yes	No
2,500 or less	4.00%	96.00%
2,501 to 6,000	11.11%	88.89%
6,001 to 14,999	0.00%	100.00%
15,000 or more	4.55%	95.45%

Table 1.17: Percentage of Colleges in the Sample that use the Assessment Package Accuplacer

	Yes	No
Entire Sample	16.67%	83.33%

Survey of Assessment Practices in Higher Education

Table 1.18: Percentage of Colleges in the Sample that use the Assessment Package Accuplacer, Broken Out by Public or Private Institutional Status

Public or Private Status	Yes	No
Public College	24.07%	75.93%
Private College	3.33%	96.67%

Table 1.19: Percentage of Colleges in the Sample that use the Assessment Package Accuplacer, Broken Out by Type of College

Type of College	Yes	No
Community College	61.54%	38.46%
Primarily a 4-year Degree Granting Institution	8.82%	91.18%
An MA or PHD Granting Institution	9.52%	90.48%
A Research University	6.25%	93.75%

Table 1.20: Percentage of Colleges in the Sample that use the Assessment Package Accuplacer, Broken Out by Full Time Equivalent Enrollment

Full Time Equivalent Enrollment	Yes	No
2,500 or less	8.00%	92.00%
2,501 to 6,000	27.78%	72.22%
6,001 to 14,999	26.32%	73.68%
15,000 or more	9.09%	90.91%

Table 1.21: Percentage of Colleges in the Sample that use the Assessment Package COMPASS

	Yes	No
Entire Sample	19.05%	80.95%

Table 1.22: Percentage of Colleges in the Sample that use the Assessment Package COMPASS, Broken Out by Type of College

Type of College	Yes	No
Community College	46.15%	53.85%
Primarily a 4-year Degree Granting Institution	20.59%	79.41%
An MA or PHD Granting Institution	14.29%	85.71%
A Research University	0.00%	100.00%

Survey of Assessment Practices in Higher Education

Table 1.23: Percentage of Colleges in the Sample that use the Assessment Package COMPASS, Broken Out by Public or Private Institutional Status

Public or Private Status	Yes	No
Public College	20.37%	79.63%
Private College	16.67%	83.33%

Table 1.24: Percentage of Colleges in the Sample that use the Assessment Package COMPASS, Broken Out by Full Time Equivalent Enrollment

Full Time Equivalent Enrollment	Yes	No
2,500 or less	20.00%	80.00%
2,501 to 6,000	22.22%	77.78%
6,001 to 14,999	21.05%	78.95%
15,000 or more	13.64%	86.36%

Table 1.25: Percentage of Colleges that Administer the Mathematics Section of COMPASS to incoming Freshmen

	Yes	No
Entire Sample	20.24%	79.76%

Table 1.26: Percentage of Colleges that Administer the Mathematics Section of COMPASS to incoming Freshmen, Broken Out by Type of College

Type of College	Yes	No
Community College	53.85%	46.15%
Primarily a 4-year Degree Granting Institution	17.65%	82.35%
An MA or PHD Granting Institution	19.05%	80.95%
A Research University	0.00%	100.00%

Table 1.27: Percentage of Colleges that Administer the Mathematics Section of COMPASS to incoming Freshmen, Broken Out by Public or Private Institutional Status

Public or Private Status	Yes	No
Public College	24.07%	75.93%
Private College	13.33%	86.67%

Survey of Assessment Practices in Higher Education

Table 1.28: Percentage of Colleges that Administer the Mathematics Section of COMPASS to incoming Freshmen, Broken Out by Full Time Equivalent Enrollment

Full Time Equivalent Enrollment	Yes	No
2,500 or less	16.00%	84.00%
2,501 to 6,000	27.78%	72.22%
6,001 to 14,999	21.05%	78.95%
15,000 or more	18.18%	81.82%

Table 1.29: Percentage of Colleges that Administer the Reading Section of COMPASS to incoming Freshmen

	Yes	No
Entire Sample	19.05%	80.95%

Table 1.30: Percentage of Colleges that Administer the Reading Section of COMPASS to incoming Freshmen, Broken Out by Type of College

Type of College	Yes	No
Community College	53.85%	46.15%
Primarily a 4-year Degree Granting Institution	20.59%	79.41%
An MA or PHD Granting Institution	9.52%	90.48%
A Research University	0.00%	100.00%

Table 1.31: Percentage of Colleges that Administer the Reading Section of COMPASS to incoming Freshmen, Broken Out by Public or Private Institutional Status

Public or Private Status	Yes	No
Public College	20.37%	79.63%
Private College	16.67%	83.33%

Table 1.32: Percentage of Colleges that Administer the Reading Section of COMPASS to incoming Freshmen, Broken Out by Full Time Equivalent Enrollment

Full Time Equivalent Enrollment	Yes	No
2,500 or less	20.00%	80.00%
2,501 to 6,000	27.78%	72.22%
6,001 to 14,999	15.79%	84.21%
15,000 or more	13.64%	86.36%

Table 1.33: Percentage of Colleges in the sample that Administer the Writing Section of COMPASS to incoming Freshmen

	Yes	No
Entire Sample	15.48%	84.52%

Table 1.34: Percentage of Colleges in the sample that Administer the Writing Section of COMPASS to incoming Freshmen, Broken Out by Type of College

Type of College	Yes	No
Community College	46.15%	53.85%
Primarily a 4-year Degree Granting Institution	14.71%	85.29%
An MA or PHD Granting Institution	9.52%	90.48%
A Research University	0.00%	100.00%

Table 1.35: Percentage of Colleges in the sample that Administer the Writing Section of COMPASS to incoming Freshmen, Broken Out by Public or Private Institutional Status

Public or Private Status	Yes	No
Public College	20.37%	79.63%
Private College	6.67%	93.33%

Table 1.36: Percentage of Colleges in the sample that Administer the Writing Section of COMPASS to incoming Freshmen, Broken Out by Full Time Equivalent Enrollment

Full Time Equivalent Enrollment	Yes	No
2,500 or less	12.00%	88.00%
2,501 to 6,000	22.22%	77.78%
6,001 to 14,999	15.79%	84.21%
15,000 or more	13.64%	86.36%

Table 1.37: Percentage of Colleges in the Sample that have ever used the NSSE

	Yes	No
Entire Sample	60.71%	39.29%

Survey of Assessment Practices in Higher Education

Table 1.38: Percentage of Colleges in the Sample that have ever used the NSSE, Broken Out by Type of College

Type of College	Yes	No
Community College	0.00%	100.00%
Primarily a 4-year Degree Granting Institution	73.53%	26.47%
An MA or PHD Granting Institution	76.19%	23.81%
A Research University	62.50%	37.50%

Table 1.39: Percentage of Colleges in the Sample that have ever used the NSSE, Broken Out by Public or Private Institutional Status

Public or Private Status	Yes	No
Public College	59.26%	40.74%
Private College	63.33%	36.67%

Table 1.40: Percentage of Colleges in the Sample that have ever used the NSSE, Broken Out by Full Time Equivalent Enrollment

Full Time Equivalent Enrollment	Yes	No
2,500 or less	48.00%	52.00%
2,501 to 6,000	61.11%	38.89%
6,001 to 14,999	73.68%	26.32%
15,000 or more	63.64%	36.36%

Table 1.41: Percentage of Colleges in the Sample that have ever used the HERI

	Yes	No
Entire Sample	33.33%	66.67%

Table 1.42: Percentage of Colleges in the Sample that have ever used the HERI, Broken Out by Type of College

Type of College	Yes	No
Community College	7.69%	92.31%
Primarily a 4-year Degree Granting Institution	44.12%	55.88%
An MA or PHD Granting Institution	33.33%	66.67%
A Research University	31.25%	68.75%

Survey of Assessment Practices in Higher Education

Table 1.43: Percentage of Colleges in the Sample that have ever used the HERI, Broken Out by Public or Private Institutional Status

Public or Private Status	Yes	No
Public College	29.63%	70.37%
Private College	40.00%	60.00%

Table 1.44: Percentage of Colleges in the Sample that have ever used the HERI, Broken Out by Full Time Equivalent Enrollment

Full Time Equivalent Enrollment	Yes	No
2,500 or less	32.00%	68.00%
2,501 to 6,000	38.89%	61.11%
6,001 to 14,999	36.84%	63.16%
15,000 or more	27.27%	72.73%

Table 1.45: Percentage of Colleges in the Sample that have ever used data from Educational Benchmarking, Inc.

	Yes	No
Entire Sample	23.81%	76.19%

Table 1.46: Percentage of Colleges in the Sample that have ever used data from Educational Benchmarking, Inc., Broken Out by Type of College

Type of College	Yes	No
Community College	7.69%	92.31%
Primarily a 4-year Degree Granting Institution	23.53%	76.47%
An MA or PHD Granting Institution	23.81%	76.19%
A Research University	37.50%	62.50%

Table 1.47: Percentage of Colleges in the Sample that have ever used data from Educational Benchmarking, Inc., Broken Out by Public or Private Institutional Status

Public or Private Status	Yes	No
Public College	31.48%	68.52%

Survey of Assessment Practices in Higher Education

Table 1.48: Percentage of Colleges in the Sample that have ever used data from Educational Benchmarking, Inc., Broken Out by Full Time Equivalent Enrollment

Full Time Equivalent Enrollment	Yes	No
2,500 or less	8.00%	92.00%
2,501 to 6,000	16.67%	83.33%
6,001 to 14,999	36.84%	63.16%
15,000 or more	36.36%	63.64%

Table 1.49: Percentage of Colleges in the Sample that have ever used the Center for Education Assessment

	Yes	No
Entire Sample	3.57%	96.43%

Table 1.50: Percentage of Colleges in the Sample that have ever used the Center for Education Assessment, Broken Out by Type of College

Type of College	Yes	No
Community College	0.00%	100.00%
Primarily a 4-year Degree Granting Institution	5.88%	94.12%
An MA or PHD Granting Institution	0.00%	100.00%
A Research University	6.25%	93.75%

Table 1.51: Percentage of Colleges in the Sample that have ever used the Center for Education Assessment, Broken Out by Public or Private Institutional Status

Public or Private Status	Yes	No
Public College	3.70%	96.30%
Private College	3.33%	96.67%

Table 1.52: Percentage of Colleges in the Sample that have ever used the Center for Education Assessment, Broken Out by Full Time Equivalent Enrollment

Full Time Equivalent Enrollment	Yes	No
2,500 or less	4.00%	96.00%
2,501 to 6,000	0.00%	100.00%
6,001 to 14,999	5.26%	94.74%
15,000 or more	4.55%	95.45%

Survey of Assessment Practices in Higher Education

Table 1.53: Percentage of Colleges in the Sample that have ever used Chalk & Wire EPortfolio

	Yes	No
Entire Sample	4.76%	95.24%

Table 1.54: Percentage of Colleges in the Sample that have ever used Chalk & Wire Eportfolio, Broken Out by Type of College

Type of College	Yes	No
Community College	15.38%	84.62%
Primarily a 4-year Degree Granting Institution	2.94%	97.06%
An MA or PHD Granting Institution	0.00%	100.00%
A Research University	6.25%	93.75%

Table 1.55: Percentage of Colleges in the Sample that have ever used Chalk & Wire Eportfolio, Broken Out by Public or Private Institutional Status

Public or Private Status	Yes	No
Public College	5.56%	94.44%
Private College	3.33%	96.67%

Table 1.56: Percentage of Colleges in the Sample that have ever used Chalk & Wire Eportfolio, Broken Out by Full Time Equivalent Enrollment

Full Time Equivalent Enrollment	Yes	No
2,500 or less	8.00%	92.00%
2,501 to 6,000	5.56%	94.44%
6,001 to 14,999	0.00%	100.00%
15,000 or more	4.55%	95.45%

Chapter 2: Standardized Testing

Table 2.1: Percentage of Colleges in the Sample that offer remedial or developmental courses in WRITING for students who do not perform well enough on standardized tests to take the normal college curriculum

	Yes	No
Entire Sample	69.05%	30.95%

Table 2.2: Percentage of Colleges in the Sample that offer remedial or developmental courses in WRITING for students who do not perform well enough on standardized tests to take the normal college curriculum, Broken Out by Type of College

Type of College	Yes	No
Community College	100.00%	0.00%
Primarily a 4-year Degree Granting Institution	64.71%	35.29%
An MA or PHD Granting Institution	71.43%	28.57%
A Research University	50.00%	50.00%

Table 2.3: Percentage of Colleges in the Sample that offer remedial or developmental courses in WRITING for students who do not perform well enough on standardized tests to take the normal college curriculum, Broken Out by Public or Private Institutional Status

Public or Private Status	Yes	No
Public College	68.52%	31.48%
Private College	70.00%	30.00%

Table 2.4: Percentage of Colleges in the Sample that offer remedial or developmental courses in WRITING for students who do not perform well enough on standardized tests to take the normal college curriculum, Broken Out by Full Time Equivalent Enrollment

Full Time Equivalent Enrollment	Yes	No
2,500 or less	56.00%	44.00%
2,501 to 6,000	33.33%	66.67%
6,001 to 14,999	31.58%	68.42%
15,000 or more	36.36%	63.64%

Survey of Assessment Practices in Higher Education

Table 2.5: Percentage of Colleges in the Sample that offer remedial or developmental courses in STUDY SKILLS for students who do not perform well enough on standardized tests to take the normal college curriculum

	Yes	No
Entire Sample	40.48%	59.52%

Table 2.6: Percentage of Colleges in the Sample that offer remedial or developmental courses in STUDY SKILLS for students who do not perform well enough on standardized tests to take the normal college curriculum, Broken Out by Type of College

Type of College	Yes	No
Community College	69.23%	30.77%
Primarily a 4-year Degree Granting Institution	44.12%	55.88%
An MA or PHD Granting Institution	28.57%	71.43%
A Research University	25.00%	75.00%

Table 2.7: Percentage of Colleges in the Sample that offer remedial or developmental courses in STUDY SKILLS for students who do not perform well enough on standardized tests to take the normal college curriculum, Broken Out by Public or Private Institutional Status

Public or Private Status	Yes	No
Public College	38.89%	61.11%
Private College	43.33%	56.67%

Table 2.8: Percentage of Colleges in the Sample that offer remedial or developmental courses in STUDY SKILLS for students who do not perform well enough on standardized tests to take the normal college curriculum, Broken Out by Full Time Equivalent Enrollment

Full Time Equivalent Enrollment	Yes	No
2,500 or less	72.00%	28.00%
2,501 to 6,000	77.78%	22.22%
6,001 to 14,999	52.63%	47.37%
15,000 or more	72.73%	27.27%

Table 2.9: Percentage of Colleges in the Sample that offer remedial or developmental courses in ENGLISH AS A SECOND LANGUAGE for students who do not perform well enough on standardized tests to take the normal college curriculum

	Yes	No
Entire Sample	38.10%	61.90%

Table 2.10: Percentage of Colleges in the Sample that offer remedial or developmental courses in ENGLISH AS A SECOND LANGUAGE for students who do not perform well enough on standardized tests to take the normal college curriculum, Broken Out by Type of College

Type of College	Yes	No
Community College	76.92%	23.08%
Primarily a 4-year Degree Granting Institution	26.47%	73.53%
An MA or PHD Granting Institution	42.86%	57.14%
A Research University	25.00%	75.00%

Table 2.11: Percentage of Colleges in the Sample that offer remedial or developmental courses in ENGLISH AS A SECOND LANGUAGE for students who do not perform well enough on standardized tests to take the normal college curriculum, Broken Out by Public or Private Institutional Status

Public or Private Status	Yes	No
Public College	42.59%	57.41%
Private College	30.00%	70.00%

Table 2.12: Percentage of Colleges in the Sample that offer remedial or developmental courses in ENGLISH AS A SECOND LANGUAGE for students who do not perform well enough on standardized tests to take the normal college curriculum, Broken Out by Full Time Equivalent Enrollment

Full Time Equivalent Enrollment	Yes	No
2,500 or less	36.00%	64.00%
2,501 to 6,000	33.33%	66.67%
6,001 to 14,999	42.11%	57.89%
15,000 or more	40.91%	59.09%

Table 2.13: Percentage of Colleges in the Sample that offer remedial or developmental courses in MATHEMATICS for students who do not perform well enough on standardized tests to take the normal college curriculum

	Yes	No
Entire Sample	67.86%	32.14%

Table 2.14: Percentage of Colleges in the Sample that offer remedial or developmental courses in MATHEMATICS for students who do not perform well enough on standardized tests to take the normal college curriculum, Broken Out by Type of College

Type of College	Yes	No
Community College	100.00%	0.00%
Primarily a 4-year Degree Granting Institution	67.65%	32.35%
An MA or PHD Granting Institution	61.90%	38.10%
A Research University	50.00%	50.00%

Table 2.15: Percentage of Colleges in the Sample that offer remedial or developmental courses in MATHEMATICS for students who do not perform well enough on standardized tests to take the normal college curriculum, Broken Out by Public or Private Institutional Status

Public or Private Status	Yes	No
Public College	72.22%	27.78%
Private College	60.00%	40.00%

Table 2.16: Percentage of Colleges in the Sample that offer remedial or developmental courses in MATHEMATICS for students who do not perform well enough on standardized tests to take the normal college curriculum, Broken Out by Full Time Equivalent Enrollment

Full Time Equivalent Enrollment	Yes	No
2,500 or less	68.00%	32.00%
2,501 to 6,000	72.22%	27.78%
6,001 to 14,999	63.16%	36.84%
15,000 or more	68.18%	31.82%

Table 2.17: Percentage of Colleges in the Sample that offer remedial or developmental courses in INFORMATION/COMPUTER LITERACY for students who do not perform well enough on standardized tests to take the normal college curriculum

	Yes	No
Entire Sample	4.76%	95.24%

Table 2.18: Percentage of Colleges in the Sample that offer remedial or developmental courses in INFORMATION/COMPUTER LITERACY for students who do not perform well enough on standardized tests to take the normal college curriculum, Broken Out by Type of College

Type of College	Yes	No
Community College	15.38%	84.62%
Primarily a 4-year Degree Granting Institution	5.88%	94.12%
An MA or PHD Granting Institution	0.00%	100.00%
A Research University	0.00%	100.00%

Table 2.19: Percentage of Colleges in the Sample that offer remedial or developmental courses in INFORMATION/COMPUTER LITERACY for students who do not perform well enough on standardized tests to take the normal college curriculum, Broken Out by Public or Private Institutional Status

Public or Private Status	Yes	No
Public College	5.56%	94.44%
Private College	3.33%	96.67%

Table 2.20: Percentage of Colleges in the Sample that offer remedial or developmental courses in INFORMATION/COMPUTER LITERACY for students who do not perform well enough on standardized tests to take the normal college curriculum, Broken Out by Full Time Equivalent Enrollment

Full Time Equivalent Enrollment	Yes	No
2,500 or less	8.00%	92.00%
2,501 to 6,000	5.56%	94.44%
6,001 to 14,999	5.26%	94.74%
15,000 or more	0.00%	100.00%

Survey of Assessment Practices in Higher Education

Table 2.21: Mean, Median, Minimum and Maximum amount that colleges in the sample spent to pay students to take standardized tests that are primarily used within the college to aid it in its assessment efforts in $U.S.

	Mean	Median	Minimum	Maximum
Entire Sample	1772.00	0.00	0.00	20000.00

Table 2.22: Mean, Median, Minimum and Maximum amount that colleges in the sample spent to pay students to take standardized tests that are primarily used within the college to aid it in its assessment efforts, in $U.S., Broken Out by Type of College

Type of College	Mean	Median	Minimum	Maximum
Community College	6.25	0.00	0.00	50.00
Primarily a 4-year Degree Granting Institution	1194.41	0.00	0.00	10000.00
An MA or PHD Granting Institution	58.33	0.00	0.00	500.00
A Research University	8333.33	7500.00	0.00	20000.00

Table 2.23: Mean, Median, Minimum and Maximum amount that colleges in the sample spent to pay students to take standardized tests that are primarily used within the college to aid it in its assessment efforts in $U.S., Broken Out by Public or Private Institutional Status

Public or Private Status	Mean	Median	Minimum	Maximum
Public College	2711.67	0.00	0.00	20000.00
Private College	362.50	0.00	0.00	5000.00

Table 2.24: Mean, Median, Minimum and Maximum amount that colleges in the sample spent to pay students to take standardized tests that are primarily used within the college to aid it in its assessment efforts in $U.S., Broken Out by Full Time Equivalent Enrollment

Full Time Equivalent Enrollment	Mean	Median	Minimum	Maximum
2,500 or less	353.33	0.00	0.00	5000.00
2,501 to 6,000	462.50	0.00	0.00	5000.00
6,001 to 14,999	3128.75	2.50	0.00	15000.00
15,000 or more	7000.00	0.00	0.00	20000.00

Table 2.25: Percentage of colleges sampled that offer a higher rate of pay or reward to students that score higher on standardized assessment tests, on the theory that this encourages full student effort

	Yes	No	We do not offer students any compensation to take the tests.	We do not conduct any such tests.
Entire Sample	1.23%	29.63%	46.91%	22.22%

Table 2.26: Percentage of colleges sampled that offer a higher rate of pay or reward to students that score higher on standardized assessment tests, on the theory that this encourages full student effort, Broken Out by Type of College

Type of College	Yes	No	We do not offer students any compensation to take the tests.	We do not conduct any such tests.
Community College	0.00%	7.69%	69.23%	23.08%
Primarily a 4-year Degree Granting Institution	0.00%	29.41%	52.94%	17.65%
An MA or PHD Granting Institution	0.00%	25.00%	50.00%	25.00%
A Research University	7.14%	57.14%	7.14%	28.57%

Table 2.27: Percentage of colleges sampled that offer a higher rate of pay or reward to students that score higher on standardized assessment tests, on the theory that this encourages full student effort, Broken Out by Public or Private Institutional Status

Public or Private Status	Yes	No	We do not offer students any compensation to take the tests.	We do not conduct any such tests.
Public College	1.96%	29.41%	47.06%	21.57%
Private College	0.00%	30.00%	46.67%	23.33%

Survey of Assessment Practices in Higher Education

Table 2.28: Percentage of colleges sampled that offer a higher rate of pay or reward to students that score higher on standardized assessment tests, on the theory that this encourages full student effort, Broken Out by Full Time Equivalent Enrollment

Full Time Equivalent Enrollment	Yes	No	We do not offer students any compensation to take the tests.	We do not conduct any such tests.
2,500 or less	0.00%	24.00%	56.00%	20.00%
2,501 to 6,000	0.00%	22.22%	50.00%	27.78%
6,001 to 14,999	5.56%	33.33%	27.78%	33.33%
15,000 or more	0.00%	40.00%	50.00%	10.00%

Chapter 3: Assessment Office

Table 3.2: Percentage of colleges that have an office of assessment or similar office or department that primarily devotes itself to assessment

	We have an office of assessment or similar department	We don't have an office or department devoted to assessment but we have an official in charge of assessment who works for another academic office or department	We don't have an official entrusted with this title or task
Entire Sample	52.38%	38.10%	9.52%

Table 3.3: Percentage of colleges that have an office of assessment or similar office or department that primarily devotes itself to assessment, Broken Out by Type of College

Type of College	We have an office of assessment or similar department	We don't have an office or department devoted to assessment but we have an official in charge of assessment who works for another academic office or department	We don't have an official entrusted with this title or task
Community College	46.15%	38.46%	15.38%
Primarily a 4-year Degree Granting Institution	55.88%	38.24%	5.88%
An MA or PHD Granting Institution	52.38%	33.33%	14.29%
A Research University	50.00%	43.75%	6.25%

Table 3.4: Percentage of colleges that have an office of assessment or similar office or department that primarily devotes itself to assessment, Broken Out by Public or Private Institutional Status

Public or Private Status	We have an office of assessment or similar department	We don't have an office or department devoted to assessment but we have an official in charge of assessment who works for another academic office or department	We don't have an official entrusted with this title or task
Public College	57.41%	31.48%	11.11%
Private College	43.33%	50.00%	6.67%

Survey of Assessment Practices in Higher Education

Table 3.5: Percentage of colleges that have an office of assessment or similar office or department that primarily devotes itself to assessment, Broken Out by Full Time Equivalent Enrollment

Full Time Equivalent Enrollment	We have an office of assessment or similar department	We don't have an office or department devoted to assessment but we have an official in charge of assessment who works for another academic office or department	We don't have an official entrusted with this title or task
2,500 or less	48.00%	44.00%	8.00%
2,501 to 6,000	44.44%	50.00%	5.56%
6,001 to 14,999	52.63%	36.84%	10.53%
15,000 or more	63.64%	22.73%	13.64%

Table 3.6: Mean, Median, Minimum and Maximum Number of Full Time Employees in the sample college's office of assessment, or similar office that is primarily devoted to this function

	Mean	Median	Minimum	Maximum
Entire Sample	1.90	1.00	0.00	13.00

Table 3.7: Mean, Median, Minimum and Maximum Number of Full Time Employees in the sample college's office of assessment, or similar office that is primarily devoted to this function, Broken Out by Type of College

Type of College	Mean	Median	Minimum	Maximum
Community College	0.75	0.75	0.00	1.50
Primarily a 4-year Degree Granting Institution	1.20	1.00	0.00	3.00
An MA or PHD Granting Institution	2.54	1.13	0.00	12.00
A Research University	3.09	2.20	0.50	13.00

Table 3.8: Mean, Median, Minimum and Maximum Number of Full Time Employees in the sample college's office of assessment, or similar office that is primarily devoted to this function, Broken Out by Public or Private Institutional Status

Public or Private Status	Mean	Median	Minimum	Maximum
Public College	2.49	1.75	0.00	13.00

Survey of Assessment Practices in Higher Education

Private College	1.06	1.00	0.00	3.00

Table 3.9: Mean, Median, Minimum and Maximum Number of Full Time Employees in the sample college's office of assessment, or similar office that is primarily devoted to this function, Broken Out by Full Time Equivalent Enrollment

Full Time Equivalent Enrollment	Mean	Median	Minimum	Maximum
2,500 or less	0.89	1.00	0.00	2.00
2,501 to 6,000	1.05	1.00	0.00	2.00
6,001 to 14,999	1.68	1.38	0.00	4.00
15,000 or more	3.78	2.70	0.50	13.00

Table 3.10: Annual salary range for the highest ranking assessment officer

	Less than $50,000	$51,000 to $60,000	$61,000 to $75,000	$76,000 to $99,000	More than $99,000
Entire Sample	16.95%	16.95%	20.34%	27.12%	18.64%

Table 3.11: Annual salary range for the highest ranking assessment officer, Broken Out by Type of College

Type of College	Less than $50,000	$51,000 to $60,000	$61,000 to $75,000	$76,000 to $99,000	More than $99,000
Community College	40.00%	10.00%	0.00%	30.00%	20.00%
Primarily a 4-year Degree Granting Institution	21.74%	26.09%	17.39%	26.09%	8.70%
An MA or PHD Granting Institution	7.14%	14.29%	35.71%	21.43%	21.43%
A Research University	0.00%	8.33%	25.00%	33.33%	33.33%

Table 3.12: Annual salary range for the highest ranking assessment officer, Broken Out by Public or Private Institutional Status

Public or Private Status	Less than $50,000	$51,000 to $60,000	$61,000 to $75,000	$76,000 to $99,000	More than $99,000
Public College	9.76%	14.63%	24.39%	26.83%	24.39%
Private College	33.33%	22.22%	11.11%	27.78%	5.56%

Survey of Assessment Practices in Higher Education

Table 3.13: Annual salary range for the highest ranking assessment officer, Broken Out by Full Time Equivalent Enrollment

Full Time Equivalent Enrollment	Less than $50,000	$51,000 to $60,000	$61,000 to $75,000	$76,000 to $99,000	More than $99,000
2,500 or less	38.89%	27.78%	16.67%	11.11%	5.56%
2,501 to 6,000	23.08%	23.08%	15.38%	23.08%	15.38%
6,001 to 14,999	0.00%	14.29%	28.57%	42.86%	14.29%
15,000 or more	0.00%	0.00%	21.43%	35.71%	42.86%

Table 3.14: Mean, Median, Minimum and Maximum size of college assessment office for colleges in the sample, in square feet

	Mean	Median	Minimum	Maximum
Entire Sample	691.28	200.00	0.00	10200.00

Table 3.15: Mean, Median, Minimum and Maximum size of college assessment office for colleges in the sample, in square feet, Broken Out by Type of College

Type of College	Mean	Median	Minimum	Maximum
Community College	731.25	400.00	125.00	2000.00
Primarily a 4-year Degree Granting Institution	214.93	145.00	0.00	700.00
An MA or PHD Granting Institution	1859.17	190.00	125.00	10200.00
A Research University	591.60	522.00	150.00	1041.00

Table 3.16: Mean, Median, Minimum and Maximum size of college assessment office for colleges in the sample, in square feet, Broken Out by Public or Private Institutional Status

Public or Private Status	Mean	Median	Minimum	Maximum
Public College	1059.00	300.00	20.00	10200.00
Private College	170.33	150.00	0.00	400.00

Table 3.17: Mean, Median, Minimum and Maximum size of college assessment office for colleges in the sample, in square feet, Broken Out by Full Time Equivalent Enrollment

Full Time Equivalent Enrollment	Mean	Median	Minimum	Maximum
2,500 or less	162.38	150.00	0.00	400.00
2,501 to 6,000	373.13	122.50	20.00	2000.00
6,001 to 14,999	445.17	400.00	150.00	1041.00
15,000 or more	1870.29	522.00	125.00	10200.00

Table 3.18: Mean, Median, Minimum and Maximum annual budget, for colleges in the sample, of the assessment office, including salaries and overhead (in $U.S.)

	Mean	Median	Minimum	Maximum
Entire Sample	195069.50	99000.00	14000.00	1400000.00

Table 3.19: Mean, Median, Minimum and Maximum annual budget, for colleges in the sample, of the assessment office, including salaries and overhead, Broken Out by Type of College

Type of College	Mean	Median	Minimum	Maximum
Community College	95000.00	120000.00	40000.00	125000.00
Primarily a 4-year Degree Granting Institution	118032.50	82795.00	14000.00	317800.00
An MA or PHD Granting Institution	749000.00	749000.00	98000.00	1400000.00
A Research University	234000.00	220000.00	80000.00	402000.00

Table 3.20: Mean, Median, Minimum and Maximum annual budget, for colleges in the sample, of the assessment office, including salaries and overhead., Broken Out by Public or Private Institutional Status

Public or Private Status	Mean	Median	Minimum	Maximum
Public College	245523.08	120000.00	40000.00	1400000.00
Private College	101370.00	85000.00	14000.00	300000.00

Survey of Assessment Practices in Higher Education

Table 3.21: Mean, Median, Minimum and Maximum annual budget, for colleges in the sample, of the assessment office, including salaries and overhead, Broken Out by Full Time Equivalent Enrollment

Full Time Equivalent Enrollment	Mean	Median	Minimum	Maximum
2,500 or less	88698.75	70295.00	14000.00	300000.00
2,501 to 6,000	94000.00	100000.00	62000.00	120000.00
6,001 to 14,999	229000.00	165000.00	120000.00	402000.00
15,000 or more	370466.67	172500.00	80000.00	1400000.00

Table 3.22: Mean, Median, Minimum and Maximum number of assessment professionals working in other offices outside of the main college assessment office

	Mean	Median	Minimum	Maximum
Entire Sample	3.10	1.00	0.00	35.00

Table 3.23: Mean, Median, Minimum and Maximum number of assessment professionals working in other offices outside of the main college assessment office, Broken Out by Type of College

Type of College	Mean	Median	Minimum	Maximum
Community College	5.72	2.00	0.00	25.00
Primarily a 4-year Degree Granting Institution	3.22	1.00	0.00	35.00
An MA or PHD Granting Institution	1.50	0.00	0.00	7.00
A Research University	2.25	1.00	0.00	7.00

Table 3.24: Mean, Median, Minimum and Maximum number of assessment professionals working in other offices outside of the main college assessment office, Broken Out by Public or Private Institutional Status

Public or Private Status	Mean	Median	Minimum	Maximum
Public College	4.52	2.00	0.00	35.00
Private College	0.77	0.00	0.00	5.00

Survey of Assessment Practices in Higher Education

Table 3.25: Mean, Median, Minimum and Maximum number of assessment professionals working in other offices outside of the main college assessment office, Broken Out by Full Time Equivalent Enrollment

Full Time Equivalent Enrollment	Mean	Median	Minimum	Maximum
2,500 or less	1.10	0.50	0.00	5.00
2,501 to 6,000	2.32	1.00	0.00	20.00
6,001 to 14,999	0.86	1.00	0.00	3.00
15,000 or more	8.43	5.00	0.00	35.00

Table 3.26: Mean, Median, Minimum and Maximum number of questions on the basic instructor evaluation form given to students

	Mean	Median	Minimum	Maximum
Entire Sample	20.62	20.00	2.00	65.00

Table 3.27: Mean, Median, Minimum and Maximum number of questions on the basic instructor evaluation form given to students, Broken Out by Type of College

Type of College	Mean	Median	Minimum	Maximum
Community College	21.60	21.50	10.00	40.00
Primarily a 4-year Degree Granting Institution	21.58	20.00	3.00	45.00
An MA or PHD Granting Institution	21.28	17.00	8.00	65.00
A Research University	16.33	19.00	2.00	25.00

Table 3.28: Mean, Median, Minimum and Maximum number of questions on the basic instructor evaluation form given to students, Broken Out by Public or Private Institutional Status

Public or Private Status	Mean	Median	Minimum	Maximum
Public College	19.17	20.00	2.00	45.00
Private College	22.72	20.00	3.00	65.00

Table 3.29: Mean, Median, Minimum and Maximum number of questions that the basic instructor evaluation form given to students, Broken Out by Full Time Equivalent Enrollment

Full Time Equivalent Enrollment	Mean	Median	Minimum	Maximum
2,500 or less	21.91	20.00	3.00	65.00
2,501 to 6,000	21.44	20.00	10.00	45.00
6,001 to 14,999	19.38	18.50	7.00	45.00
15,000 or more	19.35	20.00	2.00	40.00

Chapter 4: Student Assessment of Instructors

Table 4.1: Description of college's policies towards questionnaires for student assessment of instructors

	Not currently done at our college	Done only for a small percentage of faculty	Done for most faculty with some exceptions	Done for all faculty
Entire Sample	0.00%	2.38%	30.95%	66.67%

Table 4.2: Description of college's policies towards questionnaires for student assessment of instructors, Broken Out by Type of College

Type of College	Not currently done at our college	Done only for a small percentage of faculty	Done for most faculty with some exceptions	Done for all faculty
Community College	0.00%	7.69%	38.46%	53.85%
Primarily a 4-year Degree Granting Institution	0.00%	2.94%	32.35%	64.71%
An MA or PHD Granting Institution	0.00%	0.00%	33.33%	66.67%
A Research University	0.00%	0.00%	18.75%	81.25%

Table 4.3: Description of college's policies towards questionnaires for student assessment of instructors, Broken Out by Public or Private Institutional Status

Public or Private Status	Not currently done at our college	Done only for a small percentage of faculty	Done for most faculty with some exceptions	Done for all faculty
Public College	0.00%	3.70%	29.63%	66.67%
Private College	0.00%	0.00%	33.33%	66.67%

Survey of Assessment Practices in Higher Education

Table 4.4: Description of college's policies towards questionnaires for student assessment of instructors, Broken Out by Full Time Equivalent Enrollment

Full Time Equivalent Enrollment	Not currently done at our college	Done only for a small percentage of faculty	Done for most faculty with some exceptions	Done for all faculty
2,500 or less	0.00%	4.00%	40.00%	56.00%
2,501 to 6,000	0.00%	5.56%	27.78%	66.67%
6,001 to 14,999	0.00%	0.00%	31.58%	68.42%
15,000 or more	0.00%	0.00%	22.73%	77.27%

Table 4.5: Description of the impact of student faculty assessment questionnaires on tenure decisions

	None, really	Slight	Has some impact	Has a significant impact
Entire Sample	8.64%	14.81%	50.62%	25.93%

Table 4.6: Description of the impact of student faculty assessment questionnaires on tenure decisions, Broken Out by Type of College

Type of College	None, really	Slight	Has some impact	Has a significant impact
Community College	25.00%	16.67%	41.67%	16.67%
Primarily a 4-year Degree Granting Institution	12.12%	12.12%	48.48%	27.27%
An MA or PHD Granting Institution	0.00%	10.00%	65.00%	25.00%
A Research University	0.00%	25.00%	43.75%	31.25%

Table 4.7: Description of the impact of student faculty assessment questionnaires on tenure decisions, Broken Out by Public or Private Institutional Status

Public or Private Status	None, really	Slight	Has some impact	Has a significant impact
Public College	9.62%	13.46%	50.00%	26.92%
Private College	6.90%	17.24%	51.72%	24.14%

Survey of Assessment Practices in Higher Education

Table 4.8: Description of the impact of student faculty assessment questionnaires on tenure decisions, Broken Out by Full Time Equivalent Enrollment

Full Time Equivalent Enrollment	None, really	Slight	Has some impact	Has a significant impact
2,500 or less	12.50%	16.67%	50.00%	20.83%
2,501 to 6,000	17.65%	5.88%	58.82%	17.65%
6,001 to 14,999	5.26%	15.79%	47.37%	31.58%
15,000 or more	0.00%	19.05%	47.62%	33.33%

Table 4.9: Description of the impact of student faculty assessment questionnaires on retention decisions regarding ADJUNCT instructors

	None, really	Slight	Has some impact	Has a significant impact
Entire Sample	9.76%	15.85%	50.00%	24.39%

Table 4.10: Description of the impact of student faculty assessment questionnaires on retention decisions regarding ADJUNCT instructors, Broken Out by Type of College

Type of College	None, really	Slight	Has some impact	Has a significant impact
Community College	16.67%	25.00%	33.33%	25.00%
Primarily a 4-year Degree Granting Institution	15.15%	21.21%	39.39%	24.24%
An MA or PHD Granting Institution	0.00%	9.52%	61.90%	28.57%
A Research University	6.25%	6.25%	68.75%	18.75%

Table 4.11: Description of the impact of student faculty assessment questionnaires on retention decisions regarding ADJUNCT instructors, Broken Out by Public or Private Institutional Status

Public or Private Status	None, really	Slight	Has some impact	Has a significant impact
Public College	11.32%	13.21%	54.72%	20.75%
Private College	6.90%	20.69%	41.38%	31.03%

Table 4.12: Description of the impact of student faculty assessment questionnaires on retention decisions regarding ADJUNCT instructors, Broken Out by Full Time Equivalent Enrollment

Full Time Equivalent Enrollment	None, really	Slight	Has some impact	Has a significant impact
2,500 or less	16.67%	16.67%	37.50%	29.17%
2,501 to 6,000	5.88%	29.41%	41.18%	23.53%
6,001 to 14,999	10.53%	10.53%	52.63%	26.32%
15,000 or more	4.55%	9.09%	68.18%	18.18%

Table 4.13: Description of formats used for the completion of student assessment questionnaires

	Only in a paper format	Only in an online format	In either an online or paper format	Not offered at all at our college at this time
Entire Sample	61.90%	9.52%	27.38%	1.19%

Table 4.14: Description of formats used for the completion of student assessment questionnaires, Broken Out by Type of College

Type of College	Only in a paper format	Only in an online format	In either an online or paper format	Not offered at all at our college at this time
Community College	69.23%	15.38%	15.38%	0.00%
Primarily a 4-year Degree Granting Institution	67.65%	5.88%	23.53%	2.94%
An MA or PHD Granting Institution	61.90%	9.52%	28.57%	0.00%
A Research University	43.75%	12.50%	43.75%	0.00%

Table 4.15: Description of formats used for the completion of student assessment questionnaires, Broken Out by Public or Private Institutional Status

Public or Private Status	Only in a paper format	Only in an online format	In either an online or paper format	Not offered at all at our college at this time
Public College	53.70%	11.11%	33.33%	1.85%
Private College	76.67%	6.67%	16.67%	0.00%

Survey of Assessment Practices in Higher Education

Table 4.16: Description of formats used for the completion of student assessment questionnaires, Broken Out by Full Time Equivalent Enrollment

Full Time Equivalent Enrollment	Only in a paper format	Only in an online format	In either an online or paper format	Not offered at all at our college at this time
2,500 or less	80.00%	8.00%	12.00%	0.00%
2,501 to 6,000	55.56%	11.11%	27.78%	5.56%
6,001 to 14,999	63.16%	5.26%	31.58%	0.00%
15,000 or more	45.45%	13.64%	40.91%	0.00%

Table 4.17: Description of the impact of student course evaluations on merit pay increases for instructors

	Don't really have much of an imopact on it.	They are taken into account in merit pay decisions.	They are an important factor in merit pay decisions.
Entire Sample	53.16%	37.97%	8.86%

Table 4.18: Description of the impact of student course evaluations on merit pay increases for instructors, Broken Out by Type of College

Type of College	Don't really have much of an impact on it.	They are taken into account in merit pay decisions.	They are an important factor in merit pay decisions.
Community College	100.00%	0.00%	0.00%
Primarily a 4-year Degree Granting Institution	56.25%	34.38%	9.38%
An MA or PHD Granting Institution	36.84%	57.89%	5.26%
A Research University	31.25%	50.00%	18.75%

Table 4.19: Description of the impact of student course evaluations on merit pay increases for instructors, Broken Out by Public or Private Institutional Status

Public or Private Status	Don't really have much of an impact on it.	They are taken into account in merit pay decisions.	They are an important factor in merit pay decisions.
Public College	53.85%	36.54%	9.62%
Private College	51.85%	40.74%	7.41%

Table 4.20: Description of the impact of student course evaluations on merit pay increases for instructors, Broken Out by Full Time Equivalent Enrollment

Full Time Equivalent Enrollment	Don't really have much of an impact on it.	They are taken into account in merit pay decisions.	They are an important factor in merit pay decisions.
2,500 or less	56.52%	34.78%	8.70%
2,501 to 6,000	75.00%	18.75%	6.25%
6,001 to 14,999	50.00%	44.44%	5.56%
15,000 or more	36.36%	50.00%	13.64%

Chapter 5: Evaluation of adjunct faculty

Table 5.1: Mean, Median, Minimum and Maximum percentage of courses taught by adjunct faculty

	Mean	Median	Minimum	Maximum
Entire Sample	28.55	25.00	5.00	75.00

Table 5.2: Mean, Median, Minimum and Maximum percentage of courses taught by adjunct faculty, Broken Out by Type of College

Type of College	Mean	Median	Minimum	Maximum
Community College	46.18	50.00	25.00	65.00
Primarily a 4-year Degree Granting Institution	19.54	19.00	5.00	36.00
An MA or PHD Granting Institution	36.17	32.50	8.00	75.00
A Research University	22.89	25.00	5.00	35.00

Table 5.3: Mean, Median, Minimum and Maximum percentage of courses taught by adjunct faculty, Broken Out by Public or Private Institutional Status

Public or Private Status	Mean	Median	Minimum	Maximum
Public College	35.03	30.00	5.00	75.00
Private College	19.38	19.00	5.00	40.00

Table 5.4: Mean, Median, Minimum and Maximum percentage of courses taught by adjunct faculty, Broken Out by Full Time Equivalent Enrollment

Full Time Equivalent Enrollment	Mean	Median	Minimum	Maximum
2,500 or less	20.23	19.00	5.00	50.00
2,501 to 6,000	37.67	30.50	15.00	65.00
6,001 to 14,999	32.55	30.00	20.00	55.00
15,000 or more	30.85	30.00	5.00	75.00

Survey of Assessment Practices in Higher Education

Table 5.5: Description of the method for evaluating adjunct faculty

	Determined by the college administration	More or less left up to individual academic departments	Don't really have an official policy on this
Entire Sample	42.11%	47.37%	10.53%

Table 5.6: Description of the method for evaluating adjunct faculty, Broken Out by Type of College

Type of College	Determined by the college administration	More or less left up to individual academic departments	Don't really have an official policy on this
Community College	54.55%	36.36%	9.09%
Primarily a 4-year Degree Granting Institution	53.33%	33.33%	13.33%
An MA or PHD Granting Institution	28.57%	66.67%	4.76%
A Research University	28.57%	57.14%	14.29%

Table 5.7: Description of the method for evaluating adjunct faculty, Broken Out by Public or Private Institutional Status

Public or Private Status	Determined by the college administration	More or less left up to individual academic departments	Don't really have an official policy on this
Public College	38.00%	56.00%	6.00%
Private College	50.00%	30.77%	19.23%

Table 5.8: Description of the method for evaluating adjunct faculty, Broken Out by Full Time Equivalent Enrollment

Full Time Equivalent Enrollment	Determined by the college administration	More or less left up to individual academic departments	Don't really have an official policy on this
2,500 or less	40.91%	36.36%	22.73%
2,501 to 6,000	66.67%	26.67%	6.67%
6,001 to 14,999	26.32%	63.16%	10.53%
15,000 or more	40.00%	60.00%	0.00%

Table 5.9: Description of college's policy towards determining the evaluation of ADJUNCT instructors

	Left to each academic department to determine its policy	Policy is determined by the college administration & followed by all departments	Partially determined by the administration and partially determined by the academic departments	We really don't have a policy on this
Entire Sample	32.05%	20.51%	37.18%	10.26%

Table 5.10: Description of college's policy towards determining the evaluation of ADJUNCT instructors, Broken Out by Type of College

Type of College	Left to each academic department to determine its policy	Policy is determined by the college administration & followed by all departments	Partially determined by the administration and partially determined by the academic departments	We really don't have a policy on this
Community College	16.67%	25.00%	50.00%	8.33%
Primarily a 4-year Degree Granting Institution	19.35%	35.48%	32.26%	12.90%
An MA or PHD Granting Institution	52.38%	9.52%	33.33%	4.76%
A Research University	42.86%	0.00%	42.86%	14.29%

Table 5.11: Description of college's policy towards determining the evaluation of ADJUNCT instructors, Broken Out by Public or Private Institutional Status

Public or Private Status	Left to each academic department to determine its policy	Policy is determined by the college administration & followed by all departments	Partially determined by the administration and partially determined by the academic departments	We really don't have a policy on this
Public College	37.25%	13.73%	43.14%	5.88%
Private College	22.22%	33.33%	25.93%	18.52%

Table 5.12: Description of college's policy towards determining the evaluation of ADJUNCT instructors, Broken Out by Full Time Equivalent Enrollment

Full Time Equivalent Enrollment	Left to each academic department to determine its policy	Policy is determined by the college administration & followed by all departments	Partially determined by the administration and partially determined by the academic departments	We really don't have a policy on this
2,500 or less	26.09%	30.43%	26.09%	17.39%
2,501 to 6,000	18.75%	31.25%	37.50%	12.50%
6,001 to 14,999	36.84%	15.79%	36.84%	10.53%
15,000 or more	45.00%	5.00%	50.00%	0.00%

Table 5.13: Percentage of colleges that commonly use student evaluation forms to evaluate adjunct instructors

	Yes	No
Entire Sample	91.67%	8.33%

Table 5.14: Percentage of colleges that commonly use student evaluation forms to evaluate adjunct instructors, Broken Out by Type of College

Type of College	Yes	No
Community College	92.31%	7.69%
Primarily a 4-year Degree Granting Institution	88.24%	11.76%
An MA or PHD Granting Institution	100.00%	0.00%
A Research University	87.50%	12.50%

Table 5.15: Percentage of colleges that commonly use student evaluation forms to evaluate adjunct instructors, Broken Out by Public or Private Institutional Status

Public or Private Status	Yes	No
Public College	92.59%	7.41%
Private College	90.00%	10.00%

Survey of Assessment Practices in Higher Education

Table 5.16: Percentage of colleges that commonly use student evaluation forms to evaluate adjunct instructors, Broken Out by Full Time Equivalent Enrollment

Full Time Equivalent Enrollment	Yes	No
2,500 or less	96.00%	4.00%
2,501 to 6,000	77.78%	22.22%
6,001 to 14,999	100.00%	0.00%
15,000 or more	90.91%	9.09%

Table 5.17: Percentage of colleges that commonly use standardized tests to evaluate adjunct instructors

	Yes	No
Entire Sample	1.19%	98.81%

Table 5.18: Percentage of colleges that commonly use standardized tests to evaluate adjunct instructors, Broken Out by Type of College

Type of College	Yes	No
Community College	0.00%	100.00%
Primarily a 4-year Degree Granting Institution	2.94%	97.06%
An MA or PHD Granting Institution	0.00%	100.00%
A Research University	0.00%	100.00%

Table 5.19: Percentage of colleges that commonly use standardized tests to evaluate adjunct instructors, Broken Out by Public or Private Institutional Status

Public or Private Status	Yes	No
Public College	0.00%	100.00%
Private College	3.33%	96.67%

Table 5.20: Percentage of colleges that commonly use standardized tests to evaluate adjunct instructors, Broken Out by Full Time Equivalent Enrollment

Full Time Equivalent Enrollment	Yes	No
2,500 or less	4.00%	96.00%
2,501 to 6,000	0.00%	100.00%
6,001 to 14,999	0.00%	100.00%
15,000 or more	0.00%	100.00%

Survey of Assessment Practices in Higher Education

Table 5.21: Percentage of colleges that commonly use in class visits by full-time professors to evaluate adjunct instructors

	Yes	No
Entire Sample	59.52%	40.48%

Table 5.22: Percentage of colleges that commonly use in class visits by full-time professors to evaluate adjunct instructors, Broken Out by Type of College

Type of College	Yes	No
Community College	76.92%	23.08%
Primarily a 4-year Degree Granting Institution	50.00%	50.00%
An MA or PHD Granting Institution	71.43%	28.57%
A Research University	50.00%	50.00%

Table 5.23: Percentage of colleges that commonly use in class visits by full-time professors to evaluate adjunct instructors, Broken Out by Public or Private Institutional Status

Public or Private Status	Yes	No
Public College	57.41%	42.59%
Private College	63.33%	36.67%

Table 5.24: Percentage of colleges that commonly use in class visits by full-time professors to evaluate adjunct instructors, Broken Out by Full Time Equivalent Enrollment

Full Time Equivalent Enrollment	Yes	No
2,500 or less	68.00%	32.00%
2,501 to 6,000	66.67%	33.33%
6,001 to 14,999	52.63%	47.37%
15,000 or more	50.00%	50.00%

Table 5.25: Percentage of colleges that commonly use student evaluation forms to evaluate instructors

	Yes	No
Entire Sample	94.05%	5.95%

Survey of Assessment Practices in Higher Education

Table 5.26: Percentage of colleges that commonly use student evaluation forms to evaluate instructors, Broken Out by Type of College

Type of College	Yes	No
Community College	92.31%	7.69%
Primarily a 4-year Degree Granting Institution	91.18%	8.82%
An MA or PHD Granting Institution	100.00%	0.00%
A Research University	93.75%	6.25%

Table 5.27: Percentage of colleges that commonly use student evaluation forms to evaluate instructors, Broken Out by Public or Private Institutional Status

Public or Private Status	Yes	No
Public College	94.44%	5.56%
Private College	93.33%	6.67%

Table 5.28: Percentage of colleges that commonly use student evaluation forms to evaluate instructors, Broken Out by Full Time Equivalent Enrollment

Full Time Equivalent Enrollment	Yes	No
2,500 or less	96.00%	4.00%
2,501 to 6,000	83.33%	16.67%
6,001 to 14,999	100.00%	0.00%
15,000 or more	95.45%	4.55%

Table 5.29: Percentage of colleges that commonly use standardized tests to evaluate student learning in chosen majors

	Yes	No
Entire Sample	4.76%	95.24%

Table 5.30: Percentage of colleges that commonly use standardized tests to evaluate student learning in chosen majors, Broken Out by Type of College

Type of College	Yes	No
Community College	7.69%	92.31%
Primarily a 4-year Degree Granting Institution	2.94%	97.06%
An MA or PHD Granting Institution	9.52%	90.48%
A Research University	0.00%	100.00%

Table 5.31: Percentage of colleges that commonly use standardized tests to evaluate student learning in chosen majors, Broken Out by Public or Private Institutional Status

Public or Private Status	Yes	No
Public College	3.70%	96.30%
Private College	6.67%	93.33%

Table 5.32: Percentage of colleges that commonly use standardized tests to evaluate student learning in chosen majors, Broken Out by Full Time Equivalent Enrollment

Full Time Equivalent Enrollment	Yes	No
2,500 or less	12.00%	88.00%
2,501 to 6,000	0.00%	100.00%
6,001 to 14,999	0.00%	100.00%
15,000 or more	4.55%	95.45%

Table 5.33: Percentage of colleges that commonly use standardized tests provided by testing companies to obtain results to compare to national data

	Yes	No
Entire Sample	7.14%	92.86%

Table 5.34: Percentage of colleges that commonly use standardized tests provided by testing companies to obtain results to compare to national data to evaluate instructors, Broken Out by Type of College

Type of College	Yes	No
Community College	7.69%	92.31%
Primarily a 4-year Degree Granting Institution	8.82%	91.18%
An MA or PHD Granting Institution	9.52%	90.48%
A Research University	0.00%	100.00%

Table 5.35: Percentage of colleges that commonly use standardized tests provided by testing companies to obtain results to compare to national data, Broken Out by Public or Private Institutional Status

Public or Private Status	Yes	No
Public College	3.70%	96.30%
Private College	13.33%	86.67%

Table 5.36: Percentage of colleges that commonly use standardized tests Provided by Testing Companies to Obtain Results to Compare to National Data to evaluate instructors, Broken Out by Full Time Equivalent Enrollment

Full Time Equivalent Enrollment	Yes	No
2,500 or less	20.00%	80.00%
2,501 to 6,000	5.56%	94.44%
6,001 to 14,999	0.00%	100.00%
15,000 or more	0.00%	100.00%

Table 5.37: Percentage of colleges that commonly use In Class Visits by Full time professors or instructors or other evaluators to evaluate instructors

	Yes	No
Entire Sample	65.48%	34.52%

Table 5.38: Percentage of colleges that commonly use In Class Visits by Full time professors or instructors or other evaluators to evaluate instructors, Broken Out by Type of College

Type of College	Yes	No
Community College	84.62%	15.38%
Primarily a 4-year Degree Granting Institution	58.82%	41.18%
An MA or PHD Granting Institution	71.43%	28.57%
A Research University	56.25%	43.75%

Table 5.39: Percentage of colleges that commonly use In Class Visits by Full time professors or instructors or other evaluators to evaluate instructors, Broken Out by Public or Private Institutional Status

Public or Private Status	Yes	No
Public College	64.81%	35.19%
Private College	66.67%	33.33%

Table 5.40: Percentage of colleges that commonly use In Class Visits by Full time professors or instructors or other evaluators to evaluate instructors, Broken Out by Full Time Equivalent Enrollment

Full Time Equivalent Enrollment	Yes	No
2,500 or less	72.00%	28.00%
2,501 to 6,000	61.11%	38.89%
6,001 to 14,999	68.42%	31.58%
15,000 or more	59.09%	40.91%

Chapter 6: Faculty Involvement in Assessment

Table 6.1: Description of college faculty's role in developing the college's assessment vehicles

	It's largely an administration effort	It's led by the administration with some input from faculty	Both the college administration and faculty are intimately involved	It's been led primarily by faculty
Entire Sample	6.17%	24.69%	51.85%	17.28%

Table 6.2: Description of college faculty's role in developing the college's assessment vehicles, Broken Out by Type of College

Type of College	It's largely an administration effort	It's led by the administration with some input from faculty	Both the college administration and faculty are intimately involved	It's been led primarily by faculty
Community College	0.00%	8.33%	66.67%	25.00%
Primarily a 4-year Degree Granting Institution	12.12%	21.21%	51.52%	15.15%
An MA or PHD Granting Institution	0.00%	23.81%	57.14%	19.05%
A Research University	6.67%	46.67%	33.33%	13.33%

Table 6.3: Description of college faculty's role in developing the college's assessment vehicles, Broken Out by Public or Private Institutional Status

Public or Private Status	It's largely an administration effort	It's led by the administration with some input from faculty	Both the college administration and faculty are intimately involved	It's been led primarily by faculty
Public College	3.85%	28.85%	46.15%	21.15%
Private College	10.34%	17.24%	62.07%	10.34%

Survey of Assessment Practices in Higher Education

Table 6.4: Description of college faculty's role in developing the college's assessment vehicles, Broken Out by Full Time Equivalent Enrollment

Full Time Equivalent Enrollment	It's largely an administration effort	It's led by the administration with some input from faculty	Both the college administration and faculty are intimately involved	It's been led primarily by faculty
2,500 or less	12.00%	12.00%	64.00%	12.00%
2,501 to 6,000	6.25%	12.50%	43.75%	37.50%
6,001 to 14,999	5.26%	26.32%	47.37%	21.05%
15,000 or more	0.00%	47.62%	47.62%	4.76%

Table 6.5: Description of college faculty's views of the assessment efforts of the college administration

	For the most part faculty are suspicious of it and are not completely cooperative	Faculty pay lip service to the idea but I can't say that they are enthused about it	Faculty are on-board with most of our initiatives	Faculty are quite enthusiastic and cooperative about improving assessment at the college
Entire Sample	13.33%	48.00%	36.00%	2.67%

Table 6.6: Description of college faculty's views of the assessment efforts of the college administration, Broken Out by Type of College

Type of College	For the most part faculty are suspicious of it and are not completely cooperative	Faculty pay lip service to the idea but I can't say that they are enthused about it	Faculty are on-board with most of our initiatives	Faculty are quite enthusiastic and cooperative about improving assessment at the college
Community College	20.00%	30.00%	50.00%	0.00%
Primarily a 4-year Degree Granting Institution	12.50%	43.75%	40.63%	3.13%
An MA or PHD Granting Institution	10.00%	55.00%	35.00%	0.00%
A Research University	15.38%	61.54%	15.38%	7.69%

Survey of Assessment Practices in Higher Education

Table 6.7: Description of college faculty's views of the assessment efforts of the college administration, Broken Out by Public or Private Institutional Status

Public or Private Status	For the most part faculty are suspicious of it and are not completely cooperative	Faculty pay lip service to the idea but I can't say that they are enthused about it	Faculty are on-board with most of our initiatives	Faculty are quite enthusiastic and cooperative about improving assessment at the college
Public College	14.89%	51.06%	29.79%	4.26%
Private College	10.71%	42.86%	46.43%	0.00%

Table 6.8: Description of college faculty's views of the assessment efforts of the college administration, Broken Out by Full Time Equivalent Enrollment

Full Time Equivalent Enrollment	For the most part faculty are suspicious of it and are not completely cooperative	Faculty pay lip service to the idea but I can't say that they are enthused about it	Faculty are on-board with most of our initiatives	Faculty are quite enthusiastic and cooperative about improving assessment at the college
2,500 or less	8.33%	45.83%	45.83%	0.00%
2,501 to 6,000	20.00%	20.00%	60.00%	0.00%
6,001 to 14,999	11.11%	66.67%	11.11%	11.11%
15,000 or more	16.67%	55.56%	27.78%	0.00%

Table 6.9: Percentage of colleges in the sample that have one or more centers to develop faculty teaching skills

	Yes	No
Entire Sample	62.96%	37.04%

Table 6.10: Percentage of colleges in the sample that have one or more centers to develop faculty teaching skills, Broken Out by Type of College

Type of College	Yes	No
Community College	66.67%	33.33%
Primarily a 4-year Degree Granting Institution	48.48%	51.52%
An MA or PHD Granting Institution	61.90%	38.10%
A Research University	93.33%	6.67%

Table 6.11: Percentage of colleges in the sample that have one or more centers to develop faculty teaching skills, Broken Out by Public or Private Institutional Status

Public or Private Status	Yes	No
Public College	76.92%	23.08%
Private College	37.93%	62.07%

Table 6.12: Percentage of colleges in the sample that have one or more centers to develop faculty teaching skills, Broken Out by Full Time Equivalent Enrollment

Full Time Equivalent Enrollment	Yes	No
2,500 or less	32.00%	68.00%
2,501 to 6,000	56.25%	43.75%
6,001 to 14,999	84.21%	15.79%
15,000 or more	85.71%	14.29%

Table 6.13: Mean, Median, Minimum and Maximum approximate annual spending for staff, office space, software, and other costs for colleges in the sample that have such centers (In $ US)

	Mean	Median	Minimum	Maximum
Entire Sample	256384.62	100000.00	3000.00	1400000.00

Table 6.14: Mean, Median, Minimum and Maximum annual spending for staff, office space, software, and other costs for colleges in the sample that have such centers, Broken Out by Type of College (In $ US)

Type of College	Mean	Median	Minimum	Maximum
Community College	200000.00	200000.00	150000.00	250000.00
Primarily a 4-year Degree Granting Institution	190600.00	80000.00	3000.00	700000.00
An MA or PHD Granting Institution	70000.00	77500.00	25000.00	100000.00
A Research University	850000.00	850000.00	300000.00	1400000.00

Table 6.15: Mean, Median, Minimum and Maximum annual spending for staff, office space, software, and other costs for colleges in the sample that have such centers, Broken Out by Public or Private Institutional Status (In $ US)

Public or Private Status	Mean	Median	Minimum	Maximum
Public College	347222.22	150000.00	70000.00	1400000.00
Private College	52000.00	52500.00	3000.00	100000.00

Table 6.16: Mean, Median, Minimum and Maximum annual spending for staff, office space, software, and other costs for colleges in the sample that have such centers, Broken Out by Full Time Equivalent Enrollment (In $ US)

Full Time Equivalent Enrollment	Mean	Median	Minimum	Maximum
2,500 or less	32666.67	25000.00	3000.00	70000.00
2,501 to 6,000	80000.00	80000.00	80000.00	80000.00
6,001 to 14,999	225833.33	125000.00	75000.00	700000.00
15,000 or more	600000.00	300000.00	100000.00	1400000.00

Table 6.17: Percentages of colleges in the sample that say they have a clear policy to link instructor compensation to documented increases in teaching effectiveness

	Yes	No
Entire Sample	7.59%	92.41%

Table 6.18: Percentages of colleges in the sample that say they have a clear policy to link instructor compensation to documented increases in teaching effectiveness, Broken Out by Type of College

Type of College	Yes	No
Community College	0.00%	100.00%
Primarily a 4-year Degree Granting Institution	6.06%	93.94%
An MA or PHD Granting Institution	5.00%	95.00%
A Research University	21.43%	78.57%

Table 6.19: Percentages of colleges in the sample that say they have a clear policy to link instructor compensation to documented increases in teaching effectiveness, Broken Out by Public or Private Institutional Status

Public or Private Status	Yes	No
Public College	8.00%	92.00%
Private College	6.90%	93.10%

Table 6.20: Percentages of colleges in the sample that say they have a clear policy to link instructor compensation to documented increases in teaching effectiveness, Broken Out by Full Time Equivalent Enrollment

Full Time Equivalent Enrollment	Yes	No
2,500 or less	8.00%	92.00%
2,501 to 6,000	0.00%	100.00%
6,001 to 14,999	5.56%	94.44%
15,000 or more	15.00%	85.00%

Chapter 7: Tutoring

Table 7.1: Percentage of colleges that have a tutoring or student learning center

	Yes	No
Entire Sample	93.75%	6.25%

Table 7.2: Percentage of colleges that have a tutoring or student learning center, Broken Out by Type of College

Type of College	Yes	No
Community College	84.62%	15.38%
Primarily a 4-year Degree Granting Institution	100.00%	0.00%
An MA or PHD Granting Institution	90.00%	10.00%
A Research University	93.33%	6.67%

Table 7.3: Percentage of colleges that have a tutoring or student learning center, Broken Out by Public or Private Institutional Status

Public or Private Status	Yes	No
Public College	90.57%	9.43%
Private College	100.00%	0.00%

Table 7.4: Percentage of colleges that have a tutoring or student learning center, Broken Out by Full Time Equivalent Enrollment

Full Time Equivalent Enrollment	Yes	No
2,500 or less	100.00%	0.00%
2,501 to 6,000	88.24%	11.76%
6,001 to 14,999	89.47%	10.53%
15,000 or more	95.00%	5.00%

Table 7.5: Description of the location of the tutoring or learning center for colleges that have one

	It has its own floor or building dedicated to it	It is housed in the library	It is housed in the computer center	It's in the process of being moved or will soon be moved to the library
Entire Sample	67.74%	30.65%	0.00%	1.61%

Survey of Assessment Practices in Higher Education

Table 7.6: Description of the location of the tutoring or learning center for colleges that have one, Broken Out by Type of College

Type of College	It has its own floor or building dedicated to it	It is housed in the library	It is housed in the computer center	It's in the process of being moved or will soon be moved to the library
Community College	80.00%	20.00%	0.00%	0.00%
Primarily a 4-year Degree Granting Institution	46.15%	50.00%	0.00%	3.85%
An MA or PHD Granting Institution	85.71%	14.29%	0.00%	0.00%
A Research University	83.33%	16.67%	0.00%	0.00%

Table 7.7: Description of the location of the tutoring or learning center for colleges that have one, Broken Out by Public or Private institutional status

Public or Private Status	It has its own floor or building dedicated to it	It is housed in the library	It is housed in the computer center	It's in the process of being moved or will soon be moved to the library
Public College	72.50%	27.50%	0.00%	0.00%
Private College	59.09%	36.36%	0.00%	4.55%

Table 7.8: Description of the location of the tutoring or learning center for colleges that have one, Broken Out by Full time Equivalent Enrollment

Full Time Equivalent Enrollment	It has its own floor or building dedicated to it	It is housed in the library	It is housed in the computer center	It's in the process of being moved or will soon be moved to the library
2,500 or less	66.67%	28.57%	0.00%	4.76%
2,501 to 6,000	61.54%	38.46%	0.00%	0.00%
6,001 to 14,999	40.00%	60.00%	0.00%	0.00%
15,000 or more	88.89%	11.11%	0.00%	0.00%

Chapter 8: Assessing Student Services

Table 8.1: Percentage of colleges that survey student satisfaction with student services such as the food service, dormitory services, bookstore, library, etc.

	Yes	No
Entire Sample	87.65%	12.35%

Table 8.2: Percentage of colleges that survey student satisfaction with student services such as the food service, dormitory services, bookstore, library, etc., Broken Out by Type of College

Type of College	Yes	No
Community College	92.31%	7.69%
Primarily a 4-year Degree Granting Institution	81.25%	18.75%
An MA or PHD Granting Institution	90.48%	9.52%
A Research University	93.33%	6.67%

Table 8.3: Percentage of colleges that survey student satisfaction with student services such as the food service, dormitory services, bookstore, library, etc., Broken Out by Public or Private Institutional Status

Public or Private Status	Yes	No
Public College	90.57%	9.43%
Private College	82.14%	17.86%

Table 8.4: Percentage of colleges that survey student satisfaction with student services such as the food service, dormitory services, bookstore, library, etc., Broken Out by Full Time Equivalent Enrollment

Full Time Equivalent Enrollment	Yes	No
2,500 or less	80.00%	20.00%
2,501 to 6,000	88.24%	11.76%
6,001 to 14,999	89.47%	10.53%
15,000 or more	95.00%	5.00%

Chapter 9: Assessment Environment

Table 9.1: Percentage of colleges sampled that offer an annual "assessment day" or "assessment workshop" or "assessment seminar" or its equivalent for faculty and staff

	Yes	No
Entire Sample	30.00%	70.00%

Table 9.2: Percentage of colleges sampled that offer an annual "assessment day" or "assessment workshop" or "assessment seminar" or its equivalent for faculty and staff, Broken Out by Type of College

Type of College	Yes	No
Community College	23.08%	76.92%
Primarily a 4-year Degree Granting Institution	31.25%	68.75%
An MA or PHD Granting Institution	33.33%	66.67%
A Research University	28.57%	71.43%

Table 9.3: Percentage of colleges sampled that offer an annual "assessment day" or "assessment workshop" or "assessment seminar" or its equivalent for faculty and staff, Broken Out by Public or Private Institutional Status

Public or Private Status	Yes	No
Public College	28.85%	71.15%
Private College	32.14%	67.86%

Table 9.4: Percentage of colleges sampled that offer an annual "assessment day" or "assessment workshop" or "assessment seminar" or its equivalent for faculty and staff, Broken Out by Full Time Equivalent Enrollment

Full Time Equivalent Enrollment	Yes	No
2,500 or less	32.00%	68.00%
2,501 to 6,000	23.53%	76.47%
6,001 to 14,999	36.84%	63.16%
15,000 or more	26.32%	73.68%

Chapter 10: Curriculum Changes

Table 10.1: Description of the success of assessment efforts for colleges sampled

	Have not really led to any significant curriculum changes	Have led to some modest curriculum changes in some programs	Have led to some significant changes in some programs	Have really dramatically changed the college curriculum
Entire Sample	13.75%	43.75%	36.25%	6.25%

Table 10.2: Description of the success of assessment efforts for colleges sampled, Broken Out by Type of College

Type of College	Have not really led to any significant curriculum changes	Have led to some modest curriculum changes in some programs	Have led to some significant changes in some programs	Have really dramatically changed the college curriculum
Community College	8.33%	50.00%	25.00%	16.67%
Primarily a 4-year Degree Granting Institution	12.50%	37.50%	46.88%	3.13%
An MA or PHD Granting Institution	9.52%	52.38%	28.57%	9.52%
A Research University	26.67%	40.00%	33.33%	0.00%

Table 10.3: Description of the success of assessment efforts for colleges sampled, Broken Out by Public or Private Institutional Status

Public or Private Status	Have not really led to any significant curriculum changes	Have led to some modest curriculum changes in some programs	Have led to some significant changes in some programs	Have really dramatically changed the college curriculum
Public College	11.54%	48.08%	32.69%	7.69%
Private College	17.86%	35.71%	42.86%	3.57%

Table 10.4: Description of the success of assessment efforts for colleges sampled, Broken Out by Full Time Equivalent Enrollment

Full Time Equivalent Enrollment	Have not really led to any significant curriculum changes	Have led to some modest curriculum changes in some programs	Have led to some significant changes in some programs	Have really dramatically changed the college curriculum
2,500 or less	20.00%	32.00%	44.00%	4.00%
2,501 to 6,000	11.76%	41.18%	35.29%	11.76%
6,001 to 14,999	5.26%	57.89%	36.84%	0.00%
15,000 or more	15.79%	47.37%	26.32%	10.53%

Chapter 11: Use of Benchmarking Data

Table 11.1: Percentage of colleges sampled that have ever purchased student performance benchmarking data to compare their students' performance to that of national norms

	Yes	No
Entire Sample	43.59%	56.41%

Table 11.2: Percentage of colleges sampled that have ever purchased student performance benchmarking data to compare their students' performance to that of national norms, Broken Out by Type of College

Type of College	Yes	No
Community College	38.46%	61.54%
Primarily a 4-year Degree Granting Institution	48.39%	51.61%
An MA or PHD Granting Institution	31.58%	68.42%
A Research University	53.33%	46.67%

Table 11.3: Percentage of colleges sampled that have ever purchased student performance benchmarking data to compare their students' performance to that of national norms, Broken Out by Public or Private Institutional Status

Public or Private Status	Yes	No
Public College	47.06%	52.94%
Private College	37.04%	62.96%

Table 11.4: Percentage of colleges sampled that have ever purchased student performance benchmarking data to compare their students' performance to that of national norms, Broken Out by Full Time Equivalent Enrollment

Full Time Equivalent Enrollment	Yes	No
2,500 or less	43.48%	56.52%
2,501 to 6,000	47.06%	52.94%
6,001 to 14,999	44.44%	55.56%
15,000 or more	40.00%	60.00%

Table 11.5: Percentage of colleges sampled that use ZOOMERANG for assessment purposes

	Yes	No
Entire Sample	16.67%	83.33%

Table 11.6: Percentage of colleges sampled that use ZOOMERANG for assessment purposes, Broken Out by Type of College

Type of College	Yes	No
Community College	23.08%	76.92%
Primarily a 4-year Degree Granting Institution	20.59%	79.41%
An MA or PHD Granting Institution	14.29%	85.71%
A Research University	6.25%	93.75%

Table 11.7: Percentage of colleges sampled that use ZOOMERANG for assessment purposes, Broken Out by Public or Private Institutional Status

Public or Private Status	Yes	No
Public College	18.52%	81.48%
Private College	13.33%	86.67%

Table 11.8: Percentage of colleges sampled that use ZOOMERANG for assessment purposes, Broken Out by Full Time Equivalent Enrollment

Full Time Equivalent Enrollment	Yes	No
2,500 or less	16.00%	84.00%
2,501 to 6,000	16.67%	83.33%
6,001 to 14,999	15.79%	84.21%
15,000 or more	18.18%	81.82%

Table 11.9: Percentage of colleges sampled that use WEAVEONLINE for assessment purposes

	Yes	No
Entire Sample	3.57%	96.43%

Table 11.10: Percentage of colleges sampled that use WEAVEONLINE for assessment purposes, Broken Out by Type of College

Type of College	Yes	No
Community College	0.00%	100.00%
Primarily a 4-year Degree Granting Institution	5.88%	94.12%
An MA or PHD Granting Institution	0.00%	100.00%
A Research University	6.25%	93.75%

Survey of Assessment Practices in Higher Education

Table 11.11: Percentage of colleges sampled that use WEAVEONLINE for assessment purposes, Broken Out by Public or Private Institutional Status

Public or Private Status	Yes	No
Public College	3.70%	96.30%
Private College	3.33%	96.67%

Table 11.12: Percentage of colleges sampled that use WEAVEONLINE for assessment purposes, Broken Out by Full Time Equivalent Enrollment

Full Time Equivalent Enrollment	Yes	No
2,500 or less	4.00%	96.00%
2,501 to 6,000	0.00%	100.00%
6,001 to 14,999	10.53%	89.47%
15,000 or more	0.00%	100.00%

Table 11.13: Percentage of colleges sampled that use SURVEYMONKEY for assessment purposes

	Yes	No
Entire Sample	36.90%	63.10%

Table 11.14: Percentage of colleges sampled that use SURVEYMONKEY for assessment purposes, Broken Out by Type of College

Type of College	Yes	No
Community College	30.77%	69.23%
Primarily a 4-year Degree Granting Institution	38.24%	61.76%
An MA or PHD Granting Institution	38.10%	61.90%
A Research University	37.50%	62.50%

Table 11.15: Percentage of colleges sampled that use SURVEYMONKEY for assessment purposes, Broken Out by Public or Private Institutional Status

Public or Private Status	Yes	No
Public College	40.74%	59.26%
Private College	30.00%	70.00%

Table 11.16: Percentage of colleges sampled that use SURVEYMONKEY for assessment purposes, Broken Out by Full Time Equivalent Enrollment

Full Time Equivalent Enrollment	Yes	No
2,500 or less	28.00%	72.00%
2,501 to 6,000	33.33%	66.67%
6,001 to 14,999	36.84%	63.16%
15,000 or more	50.00%	50.00%

Table 11.17: Percentage of colleges sampled that use WEBSURVEYOR for assessment purposes

	Yes	No
Entire Sample	9.52%	90.48%

Table 11.18: Percentage of colleges sampled that use WEBSURVEYOR for assessment purposes, Broken Out by Type of College

Type of College	Yes	No
Community College	7.69%	92.31%
Primarily a 4-year Degree Granting Institution	5.88%	94.12%
An MA or PHD Granting Institution	14.29%	85.71%
A Research University	12.50%	87.50%

Table 11.19: Percentage of colleges sampled that use WEBSURVEYOR for assessment purposes, Broken Out by Public or Private Institutional Status

Public or Private Status	Yes	No
Public College	14.81%	85.19%
Private College	0.00%	100.00%

Table 11.20: Percentage of colleges sampled that use WEBSURVEYOR for assessment purposes, Broken Out by Full Time Equivalent Enrollment

Full Time Equivalent Enrollment	Yes	No
2,500 or less	0.00%	100.00%
2,501 to 6,000	11.11%	88.89%
6,001 to 14,999	10.53%	89.47%
15,000 or more	18.18%	81.82%

Survey of Assessment Practices in Higher Education

Table 11.21: Percentage of colleges sampled that use STUDENTVOICE for assessment purposes

	Yes	No
Entire Sample	2.38%	97.62%

Table 11.22: Percentage of colleges sampled that use STUDENTVOICE for assessment purposes, Broken Out by Type of College

Type of College	Yes	No
Community College	0.00%	100.00%
Primarily a 4-year Degree Granting Institution	5.88%	94.12%
An MA or PHD Granting Institution	0.00%	100.00%
A Research University	0.00%	100.00%

Table 11.23: Percentage of colleges sampled that use STUDENTVOICE for assessment purposes, Broken Out by Public or Private Institutional Status

Public or Private Status	Yes	No
Public College	1.85%	98.15%
Private College	3.33%	96.67%

Table 11.24: Percentage of colleges sampled that use STUDENTVOICE for assessment purposes, Broken Out by Full Time Equivalent Enrollment

Full Time Equivalent Enrollment	Yes	No
2,500 or less	0.00%	100.00%
2,501 to 6,000	5.56%	94.44%
6,001 to 14,999	0.00%	100.00%
15,000 or more	4.55%	95.45%

Table 11.25: Percentage of colleges sampled that use KEY SURVEY for assessment purposes

	Yes	No
Entire Sample	1.19%	98.81%

Table 11.26: Percentage of colleges sampled that use KEY SURVEY for assessment purposes, Broken Out by Type of College

Type of College	Yes	No
Community College	7.69%	92.31%
Primarily a 4-year Degree Granting Institution	0.00%	100.00%
An MA or PHD Granting Institution	0.00%	100.00%
A Research University	0.00%	100.00%

Table 11.27: Percentage of colleges sampled that use KEY SURVEY for assessment purposes, Broken Out by Public or Private Institutional Status

Public or Private Status	Yes	No
Public College	1.85%	98.15%
Private College	0.00%	100.00%

Table 11.28: Percentage of colleges sampled that use KEY SURVEY for assessment purposes, Broken Out by Full Time Equivalent Enrollment

Full Time Equivalent Enrollment	Yes	No
2,500 or less	0.00%	100.00%
2,501 to 6,000	0.00%	100.00%
6,001 to 14,999	0.00%	100.00%
15,000 or more	4.55%	95.45%

Table 11.29: Percentage of colleges sampled that use SURVEY TRACKER PLUS for assessment purposes

	Yes	No
Entire Sample	2.38%	97.62%

Table 11.30: Percentage of colleges sampled that use SURVEY TRACKER PLUS for assessment purposes, Broken Out by Type of College

Type of College	Yes	No
Community College	15.38%	84.62%
Primarily a 4-year Degree Granting Institution	0.00%	100.00%
An MA or PHD Granting Institution	0.00%	100.00%
A Research University	0.00%	100.00%

Table 11.31: Percentage of colleges sampled that use SURVEY TRACKER PLUS for assessment purposes, Broken Out by Public or Private Institutional Status

Public or Private Status	Yes	No
Public College	3.70%	96.30%
Private College	0.00%	100.00%

Table 11.32: Percentage of colleges sampled that use SURVEY TRACKER PLUS for assessment purposes, Broken Out by Full Time Equivalent Enrollment

Full Time Equivalent Enrollment	Yes	No
2,500 or less	0.00%	100.00%
2,501 to 6,000	0.00%	100.00%
6,001 to 14,999	5.26%	94.74%
15,000 or more	4.55%	95.45%

Table 11.33: Percentage of colleges sampled that use SNAP for assessment purposes

	Yes	No
Entire Sample	4.76%	95.24%

Table 11.34: Percentage of colleges sampled that use SNAP for assessment purposes, Broken Out by Type of College

Type of College	Yes	No
Community College	7.69%	92.31%
Primarily a 4-year Degree Granting Institution	5.88%	94.12%
An MA or PHD Granting Institution	4.76%	95.24%
A Research University	0.00%	100.00%

Table 11.35: Percentage of colleges sampled that use SNAP for assessment purposes, Broken Out by Public or Private Institutional Status

Public or Private Status	Yes	No
Public College	5.56%	94.44%
Private College	3.33%	96.67%

Survey of Assessment Practices in Higher Education

Table 11.36: Percentage of colleges sampled that use SNAP for assessment purposes, Broken Out by Full Time Equivalent Enrollment

Full Time Equivalent Enrollment	Yes	No
2,500 or less	4.00%	96.00%
2,501 to 6,000	11.11%	88.89%
6,001 to 14,999	0.00%	100.00%
15,000 or more	4.55%	95.45%

Table 11.37: Percentage of colleges sampled that use FLASHLIGHT ONLINE for assessment purposes

	Yes	No
Entire Sample	5.95%	94.05%

Table 11.38: Percentage of colleges sampled that use FLASHLIGHT ONLINE for assessment purposes, Broken Out by Type of College

Type of College	Yes	No
Community College	7.69%	92.31%
Primarily a 4-year Degree Granting Institution	8.82%	91.18%
An MA or PHD Granting Institution	0.00%	100.00%
A Research University	6.25%	93.75%

Table 11.39: Percentage of colleges sampled that use FLASHLIGHT ONLINE for assessment purposes, Broken Out by Public or Private Institutional Status

Public or Private Status	Yes	No
Public College	5.56%	94.44%
Private College	6.67%	93.33%

Table 11.40: Percentage of colleges sampled that use FLASHLIGHT ONLINE for assessment purposes, Broken Out by Full Time Equivalent Enrollment

Full Time Equivalent Enrollment	Yes	No
2,500 or less	8.00%	92.00%
2,501 to 6,000	5.56%	94.44%
6,001 to 14,999	0.00%	100.00%
15,000 or more	9.09%	90.91%

Survey of Assessment Practices in Higher Education

Table 11.41: Percentage of colleges sampled that use ULTIMATE SURVEY for assessment purposes

	Yes	No
Entire Sample	2.38%	97.62%

Table 11.42: Percentage of colleges sampled that use ULTIMATE SURVEY for assessment purposes, Broken Out by Type of College

Type of College	Yes	No
Community College	0.00%	100.00%
Primarily a 4-year Degree Granting Institution	5.88%	94.12%
An MA or PHD Granting Institution	0.00%	100.00%
A Research University	0.00%	100.00%

Table 11.43: Percentage of colleges sampled that use ULTIMATE SURVEY for assessment purposes, Broken Out by Public or Private Institutional Status

Public or Private Status	Yes	No
Public College	3.70%	96.30%
Private College	0.00%	100.00%

Table 11.44: Percentage of colleges sampled that use ULTIMATE SURVEY for assessment purposes, Broken Out by Full Time Equivalent Enrollment

Full Time Equivalent Enrollment	Yes	No
2,500 or less	0.00%	100.00%
2,501 to 6,000	5.56%	94.44%
6,001 to 14,999	5.26%	94.74%
15,000 or more	0.00%	100.00%

Chapter 12: Use of Consultants and Services

Table 12.1: Mean, Median, Minimum and Maximum spending by the college administration on outside consultants, reports, conferences and other consulting services related to assessment within the past year (in $U.S.)

	Mean	Median	Minimum	Maximum
Entire Sample	12984.38	5000.00	0.00	75000.00

Table 12.2: Mean, Median, Minimum and Maximum spending by the college administration on outside consultants, reports, conferences and other consulting services related to assessment within the past year, Broken Out by Type of College (in $U.S.)

Type of College	Mean	Median	Minimum	Maximum
Community College	27083.33	30000.00	0.00	50000.00
Primarily a 4-year Degree Granting Institution	13571.43	5000.00	0.00	75000.00
An MA or PHD Granting Institution	5714.29	5000.00	0.00	15000.00
A Research University	4600.00	5000.00	0.00	10000.00

Table 12.3: Mean, Median, Minimum and Maximum spending by the college administration on outside consultants, reports, conferences and other consulting services related to assessment within the past year, Broken Out by Public or Private Institutional Status (in $U.S.)

Public or Private Status	Mean	Median	Minimum	Maximum
Public College	15100.00	5000.00	0.00	75000.00
Private College	9458.33	7000.00	0.00	28000.00

Table 12.4: Mean, Median, Minimum and Maximum spending by the college administration on outside consultants, reports, conferences and other consulting services related to assessment within the past year, Broken Out by Full Time Equivalent Enrollment (in $U.S.)

Full Time Equivalent Enrollment	Mean	Median	Minimum	Maximum
2,500 or less	10833.33	5000.00	0.00	50000.00
2,501 to 6,000	13250.00	7500.00	0.00	50000.00
6,001 to 14,999	19285.71	5000.00	0.00	75000.00
15,000 or more	6000.00	6000.00	2000.00	10000.00

Table 12.5: Mean, Median, Minimum and Maximum approximate number of conferences devoted to assessment issues that ADMINISTRATORS from colleges surveyed attended in the past year

	Mean	Median	Minimum	Maximum
Entire Sample	2.58	2.50	0.00	10.00

Table 12.6: Mean, Median, Minimum and Maximum approximate number of conferences devoted to assessment issues that ADMINISTRATORS from colleges surveyed attended in the past year, Broken Out by Type of College

Type of College	Mean	Median	Minimum	Maximum
Community College	2.50	3.00	1.00	3.00
Primarily a 4-year Degree Granting Institution	2.57	2.00	0.00	10.00
An MA or PHD Granting Institution	2.83	3.00	0.00	5.00
A Research University	2.33	2.00	0.00	4.00

Table 12.7: Mean, Median, Minimum and Maximum approximate number of conferences devoted to assessment issues that ADMINISTRATORS from colleges surveyed attended in the past year, Broken Out by Public or Private Institutional Status

Public or Private Status	Mean	Median	Minimum	Maximum
Public College	2.91	3.00	0.00	10.00
Private College	1.94	2.00	0.00	3.00

Table 12.8: Mean, Median, Minimum and Maximum approximate number of conferences devoted to assessment issues that ADMINISTRATORS from colleges surveyed attended in the past year, Broken Out by Full Time Equivalent Enrollment

Full Time Equivalent Enrollment	Mean	Median	Minimum	Maximum
2,500 or less	2.00	2.00	0.00	3.00
2,501 to 6,000	1.85	2.00	0.00	3.00
6,001 to 14,999	3.18	3.00	2.00	5.00
15,000 or more	3.73	3.00	0.00	10.00

Chapter 13: Post Graduation Assessment

When survey participants were asked to describe the scope and detail of the college's post graduate assessment program nearly all who responded mentioned the use of alumni or graduate surveys. Also mentioned was the use of employer surveys.

Table 13.1: Percentage of colleges surveyed that have a post graduate assessment program

	Yes	No
Entire Sample	36.99%	63.01%

Table 13.2: Percentage of colleges surveyed that have a post graduate assessment program, Broken Out by Type of College

Type of College	Yes	No
Community College	25.00%	75.00%
Primarily a 4-year Degree Granting Institution	38.71%	61.29%
An MA or PHD Granting Institution	37.50%	62.50%
A Research University	42.86%	57.14%

Table 13.3: Percentage of colleges surveyed that have a post graduate assessment program, Broken Out by Public or Private Institutional Status

Public or Private Status	Yes	No
Public College	37.50%	62.50%
Private College	36.00%	64.00%

Table 13.4: Percentage of colleges surveyed that have a post graduate assessment program, Broken Out by Full Time Equivalent Enrollment

Full Time Equivalent Enrollment	Yes	No
2,500 or less	33.33%	66.67%
2,501 to 6,000	26.67%	73.33%
6,001 to 14,999	37.50%	62.50%
15,000 or more	50.00%	50.00%

Table 13.5: Percentage of colleges surveyed that at least once per year conduct INTERVIEWS OF STUDENTS WHO GRADUATE

	Yes	No
Entire Sample	34.52%	65.48%

Survey of Assessment Practices in Higher Education

Table 13.6: Percentage of colleges surveyed that conduct at least once per year INTERVIEWS OF STUDENTS WHO GRADUATE, Broken Out by Type of College

Type of College	Yes	No
Community College	30.77%	69.23%
Primarily a 4-year Degree Granting Institution	47.06%	52.94%
An MA or PHD Granting Institution	23.81%	76.19%
A Research University	25.00%	75.00%

Table 13.7: Percentage of colleges surveyed that conduct at least once per year INTERVIEWS OF STUDENTS WHO GRADUATE, Broken Out By Public or Private Institutional Status

Public or Private Status	Yes	No
Public College	35.19%	64.81%
Private College	33.33%	66.67%

Table 13.8: Percentage of colleges surveyed that conduct INTERVIEWS OF STUDENTS WHO GRADUATE at least once per year, Broken Out by Full Time Equivalent Enrollment

Full Time Equivalent Enrollment	Yes	No
2,500 or less	44.00%	56.00%
2,501 to 6,000	27.78%	72.22%
6,001 to 14,999	36.84%	63.16%
15,000 or more	27.27%	72.73%

Table 13.9: Percentage of colleges surveyed that conduct at least once per year INTERVIEWS OF STUDENTS WHO TRANSFER OUT OF COLLEGE

	Yes	No
Entire Sample	23.53%	75.29%

Table 13.10: Percentage of colleges surveyed that conduct at least once per year INTERVIEWS OF STUDENTS WHO TRANSFER OUT OF COLLEGE, Broken Out by Type of College

Type of College	Yes	No
Community College	15.38%	84.62%
Primarily a 4-year Degree Granting Institution	35.29%	64.71%
An MA or PHD Granting Institution	23.81%	76.19%
A Research University	6.25%	93.75%

Table 13.11: Percentage of colleges surveyed that conduct at least once per year INTERVIEWS OF STUDENTS WHO TRANSFER OUT OF COLLEGE, Broken Out by Public or Private Institutional Status

Public or Private Status	Yes	No
Public College	18.52%	81.48%
Private College	33.33%	66.67%

Table 13.12: Percentage of colleges surveyed that conduct at least once per year INTERVIEWS OF STUDENTS WHO TRANSFER OUT OF COLLEGE, Broken Out by Full Time Equivalent Enrollment

Full Time Equivalent Enrollment	Yes	No
2,500 or less	40.00%	60.00%
2,501 to 6,000	27.78%	72.22%
6,001 to 14,999	5.26%	94.74%
15,000 or more	18.18%	81.82%

Table 13.13: Percentage of colleges surveyed that conduct at least once per year INTERVIEWS OF STUDENTS WHO DROP OUT OF COLLEGE

	Yes	No
Entire Sample	29.41%	69.41%

Survey of Assessment Practices in Higher Education

Table 13.14: Percentage of colleges surveyed that conduct at least once per year INTERVIEWS OF STUDENTS WHO DROP OUT OF THE COLLEGE, Broken Out by Type of College

Type of College	Yes	No
Community College	30.77%	69.23%
Primarily a 4-year Degree Granting Institution	41.18%	58.82%
An MA or PHD Granting Institution	28.57%	71.43%
A Research University	6.25%	93.75%

Table 13.15: Percentage of colleges surveyed that conduct at least once per year INTERVIEWS OF STUDENTS WHO DROP OUT OF THE COLLEGE, Broken Out by Public or Private Institutional Status

Public or Private Status	Yes	No
Public College	22.22%	77.78%
Private College	43.33%	56.67%

Table 13.16: Percentage of colleges surveyed that conduct at least once per year INTERVIEWS OF STUDENTS WHO DROP OUT OF THE COLLEGE, Broken Out by Full Time Equivalent Enrollment

Full Time Equivalent Enrollment	Yes	No
2,500 or less	52.00%	48.00%
2,501 to 6,000	33.33%	66.67%
6,001 to 14,999	10.53%	89.47%
15,000 or more	18.18%	81.82%

Table 13.17: Mean, Median, Minimum and Maximum approximate number of exit interviews conducted with graduating students

	Mean	Median	Minimum	Maximum
Entire Sample	1117.64	87.50	0.00	10000.00

Table 13.18: Mean, Median, Minimum and Maximum approximate number of exit interviews conducted with graduating students, Broken Out by Type of College

Type of College	Mean	Median	Minimum	Maximum
Community College	938.50	938.50	25.00	1852.00
Primarily a 4-year Degree Granting Institution	475.00	100.00	50.00	2400.00
An MA or PHD Granting Institution	150.00	150.00	0.00	300.00
A Research University	3381.67	75.00	70.00	10000.00

Table 13.19: Mean, Median, Minimum and Maximum approximate number of exit interviews conducted with graduating students, Broken Out by Public or Private Institutional Status

Public or Private Status	Mean	Median	Minimum	Maximum
Public College	1489.70	87.50	0.00	10000.00
Private College	187.50	150.00	50.00	400.00

Table 13.20: Mean, Median, Minimum and Maximum approximate number of exit interviews conducted with graduating students, Broken Out by Full Time Equivalent Enrollment

Full Time Equivalent Enrollment	Mean	Median	Minimum	Maximum
2,500 or less	164.00	70.00	50.00	400.00
2,501 to 6,000	66.67	75.00	25.00	100.00
6,001 to 14,999	1350.00	1350.00	300.00	2400.00
15,000 or more	2981.75	963.50	0.00	10000.00

Table 13.21: Mean, Median, Minimum and Maximum approximate number of exit interviews conducted with students who left the college for any reason in the past year

	Mean	Median	Minimum	Maximum
Entire Sample	129.31	45.00	0.00	1280.00

We asked for but did not receive enough data to run the above data by type of college.

Table 13.22: Mean, Median, Minimum and Maximum approximate number of exit interviews conducted with students who left the college for any reason in the past year, Broken Out by Public or Private Institutional Status

Public or Private Status	Mean	Median	Minimum	Maximum
Public College	259.17	62.50	0.00	1280.00
Private College	51.40	45.00	0.00	100.00

Table 13.23: Mean, Median, Minimum and Maximum approximate number of exit interviews conducted with students who left the college for any reason in the past year, Broken Out by Full Time Equivalent Enrollment

Full Time Equivalent Enrollment	Mean	Median	Minimum	Maximum
2,500 or less	53.00	51.00	0.00	100.00
2,501 to 6,000	73.00	50.00	25.00	150.00
6,001 to 14,999	0.00	0.00	0.00	0.00
15,000 or more	640.00	640.00	0.00	1280.00

Table 13.24: Percentage of colleges that offer compensation of any kind for students that take exit interviews

	Yes	No
Entire Sample	3.70%	96.30%

Table 13.25: Percentage of colleges that offer compensation of any kind for students that take exit interviews, Broken Out by Type of College

Type of College	Yes	No
Community College	0.00%	100.00%
Primarily a 4-year Degree Granting Institution	0.00%	100.00%
An MA or PHD Granting Institution	14.29%	85.71%
A Research University	0.00%	100.00%

Table 13.26: Percentage of colleges that offer compensation of any kind for students that take exit interviews, Broken Out by Public or Private Institutional Status

Public or Private Status	Yes	No
Public College	5.26%	94.74%
Private College	0.00%	100.00%

Table 13.27: Percentage of colleges that offer compensation of any kind for students that take exit interviews, Broken Out by Full Time Equivalent Enrollment

Full Time Equivalent Enrollment	Yes	No
2,500 or less	0.00%	100.00%
2,501 to 6,000	9.09%	90.91%
6,001 to 14,999	9.09%	90.91%
15,000 or more	0.00%	100.00%

Chapter 14: Assessing Assessment

We asked administrators in charge of assessment at various colleges to provide some examples of instances when assessment procedures revealed student or program deficiencies, how those deficiencies were addressed, and what the were the results of these efforts.

1. We have added extra math courses into the mathematics major. We have restructured our testing procedure and remedial courses to better meet students' needs. Overlapping courses were restructured or discontinued. More choices were given in general education.
2. MFAT in Business revealed weakness in an academic discipline - textbook changed; better results.
3. Student evaluations reveal dissatisfaction with community service requirement - process changed; results pending.
4. The results of our Non-Completer Phone Survey have prompted us to pay closer attention to some of the departments students encounter first (e.g., Advising, Placement Testing Center). As a result, policies and procedures have changed dramatically.
5. Examination of exit portfolios in the education department led to creation of some new assignments required for majors to meet state standards.
6. Assessment of the number of students failing introductory science courses has led to an initiative looking at revamping all introductory science courses for non-science majors.
7. Inconsistent results from students taking the Accuplacer have led to a restructuring of curriculum in math, reading, and English developmental courses.
8. Using alumni survey data showed students not well prepared in some outcomes. Faculty have revised parts of the curriculum to address these. Students not performing well on project report writing as seen in student work. Changes in teaching methods to address this. Student not performing well on certain topics in external licensure exams. Curriculum changes to address these weaknesses.
9. In our general education assessment, the expectations for oral and written presentations were not met. A greater emphasis of professionalism during those reports has ensued, and all faculty in all departments are making the students aware of the higher standards.
10. Started assessment this year. In pilot, found lack of sufficient time spent on certain outcomes through required courses. Are now reviewing the curriculum to make changes to required classes to ensure sufficient coverage of the desired outcomes. Results to be determined in several years after changes have been implemented and students progress through the new curriculum.
11. Biology students quantitative skills needed to be improved, consequently an entirely new math course with Bio data samples was implemented.
12. Indirect and direct evidence of general education areas such as student writing samples, capstone projects, critical thinking assessments and information literacy assessments, and data from NSSE and SSI led to a redesign of the college general education curriculum. Assessment in progress.
13. Post-course interviews with seniors revealed that we needed to combine learning and cognition courses. Post-course questionnaires revealed low student interest (and some fear) toward research, which led to restructuring of the research sequence.
14. Math majors scored low on the senior major field test. A capstone course was added to review math concepts learned earlier. Scores greatly improved.

Survey of Assessment Practices in Higher Education

15. Data indicated that students were not performing well on the Math Compass. This information was shared with the Math Dept, who has since developed steps to address the teaching in learning in the department.
16. NSSE revealed inadequate interaction between faculty and students. The First Year Experience program established several initiatives to increase interaction. Assessment of academic improvement of students who used tutorial services indicated that African American students who used tutorial services did not perform as well as their counterparts. This led to the design of focus groups to ascertain reason for the differences. Study has not been completed.
17. Oral communication competency assessment for undergraduates revealed competence but not enough high competency. Recommendations were made to the provost but not implemented.
18. Several assessments indicated a need for improvement in advising, so several campuses have hired additional advisors and changed their advising procedures and are seeing improvements. Remedial math courses have been added and/or modified in an effort to improve the success of students in math.
19. Frosh Writing Seminar Assessment of student essays. Randomly selected the first assignment of the fall semester and the last research assignment of Spring Semester. We graded via a holistic rubric and a features rubric for each paper. We discovered students second semester did not get sufficient research and writing instruction. We made a summary report to whole faculty, did faculty development for the professors of spring semester, and instituted a pilot program of research instruction. We have followed through with faculty development and result-oriented information dissemination. The second and third assessment of this program showed significant improvement.
20. Mathematics department discovered that the content in Intermediate Algebra and College Algebra didn't connect the two courses together as a result of embedded questions on final exam. The faculty changed the content in Intermediate Algebra to correct this problem. All other findings have just been discovered and thus improvements are not available at this time.
21. Assessment focused on writing has led to curricular revision in the writing program. Assessment of students' familiarity with religious material has led to some revision of curriculum in biblical studies.
22. In the Graduation Writing Assessment Requirement a faculty task-force, led by Comp faculty, identified a mis-fit between curriculum/instruction and the timed-essay exam used as a graduation barrier. We took the problem to the Faculty Senate and provided a solution consisting of (a) smoother sequencing of the undergraduate writing curriculum and (b) changing the exam into a placement test for upper-division writing courses. The Faculty Senate voted the change in; now Comp faculty are working on instituting the changes, to include an exam with a task more appropriate to students from across all disciplines, a new rubric for scoring the exam that comprises writing skills more appropriate to writers from all disciplines, and additional adjunct course/tutorial support for students identified as needing more help. The comp faculty continues to work on replacing the timed-essay exam with a portfolio evaluation.
23. We have many, many examples; here are a few: We completely sunseted our earlier Liberal Studies program, because we could not demonstrate learning gains despite years of effort. We completely transformed the program with new goals and objectives, and then designed courses to meet those objectives, and we now monitor the program every year to track student growth and development. We now see meaningful gains in student learning with our new program. 2. We have discontinued programs as a result of poor assessment results. Of course, no decision was made solely on the basis of assessment outcomes; there are always other resource issues in play. 3. We have restructured

Survey of Assessment Practices in Higher Education

programs as a result of important assessment results: example: Fashion Merchandising is a minor now, not a major. It is now located in the College of Business. 4. Several programs have restructured their majors as a result of assessment data. Psychology courses re-sequenced to present required research and statistics early in the program. There are so many other examples we could provide. We have been engaged in active assessment for well over 20 years. We have two formal Assessment Days each year with required student participation. We are serious about assessment and demand excellence in data collection strategies and psychometrics.

24. Usually programs work on assignment revisions for greater alignment in concert with sharpening of criteria. This is done in collaboration with assessment consultants in CTLT; my unit.
25. We recently completed a year-long self-study called Foundations of Excellence in order to improve the first year experience. Deficiencies were illuminated in 7 basic areas. Among these was advising, and professional development on advising. The advising process was changed to make it more faculty-driven and advising professional development was developed and conducted. A new position was created to provide a faculty liaison.
26. One example: a department discovered, via analysis of products students generated in a capstone course, that students were not integrating curricular content from their various courses -- they changed aspects of their undergrad curriculum and also revised the capstone course itself, including adding a team-teaching component.
27. Assessment of student learning outcomes has led to some teaching or curriculum changes in some departments. Results of changes have not been reported yet.
28. Too numerous to detail - assessment woven into all professional schools and some A&S units
29. Survey results indicated that graduates were not familiar with alumni benefits. This was addressed with an alumni database and regular communications to alumni about benefits.
30. The English department was not pleased with students' abilities to utilize MLA guidelines. They spent significant class time on addressing this issue which resulted in very significant improvements.
31. "Benchmark assessments have improved content delivery and alignment of standards within courses. Faculty reviewed program effectiveness in august and have implemented ways to improve student learning outcomes related to a culturally diverse perspective. In addition, the alignment of standards resulted in changes to the early childhood program." - College of Education Annual Report 2005-2006
32. 1. In a senior level ethics course, students were not incorporating major ethical theories into the research papers they wrote for the class. The instructor incorporated a mid-term exam which required students to use the theories in a case study. When that was done, a majority of the students in the class incorporated a major ethical theory into their research papers. 2. Students in social work were getting low scores in research in the ACAT test in Social Work, which is their senior test. The department changed instructors to a faculty member who was more highly trained in research and the students' research scores improved significantly. 3. A psychology professor was not happy with the low scores students were getting on tests in one of her courses. She added periodic quizzes between the exams and students test scores improved significantly.
33. Program review processes result in departmental reconsideration of curriculum, degree design, recruitment and retention processes and more.
34. Looking at student work from the same course across instructors prompted some programs to develop "non-negotiable" core assignments that can be used to provide evidence of key program outcomes. We are also moving to adopt an e-portfolio tool that will facilitate collection and rating of student work, as well as data aggregation.

Survey of Assessment Practices in Higher Education

35. Sociology department discovered student deficiencies in using statistical methods and completely reworked their course sequence to assist students in mastering the use of statistics in their research projects.
36. In several departments, courses with high DFW rates were examined and modified. For example, Human Anatomy and Physiology was a single course, but has been separated into two courses as a result of assessment procedures. In the Art Department, the entire course of study was revised as a result of assessment procedures and additional courses were added to the major. In both of these cases, as well as in other situations across campus, student achievement has improved dramatically.

Other Reports from Primary Research Group, Inc.

COLLEGE ALUMNI RELATIONS BENCHMARKS
Price: $295.00   Publication Date: 2007
This report gives critical data about the alumni relations efforts of North American colleges. In more than 115 pages and 400 tables, the study presents hard data on alumni affairs' office budgets, marketing expenditures, use of print publications and the Internet, directory building and fundraising activities, among other topics. The report, based on data from 60 colleges, gives the end-user highly specific benchmarking data such as the percentage of alumni that participate in reunions, earning from insurance plans and credit cards offered to alumni, spending on promotional materials for alumni clubs, percentage of alumni for whom the college maintains a working email address, and hundreds of other useful benchmarks and data points. Useful benchmarks include alumni office staff size, staff time spent on specific tasks, impact of the Internet on alumni communications, relations with the Office of Institutional Advancement, plans for the print directory and much more. Data are broken out for public and private colleges and by size and type of college and by size of the overall alumni population.

THE SURVEY OF DISTANCE LEARNING PROGRAMS IN HIGHER EDUCATION, 2007-08 EDITION
ISBN: 1-57440-087-8   Price: $129.50
The study is based on data from 45 higher education distance learning programs, with mean revenues of approximately $2.35 million. Data are broken out by size and type of college, for public and private colleges and for high, medium and low growth enrollment distance learning programs. The 200-page report presents more than 750 tables of data exploring many facets of distance learning programs, including revenues, cost structure, rates of pay, student demographics, program growth rates, current and planned use of new technologies, catering to special populations, and many other financial and business aspects of managing distance learning programs.

THE SURVEY OF COLLEGE MARKETING PROGRAMS
Price: $265.00   Publication Date: 2007
This report is based on detailed interviews with 55 American colleges. The report presents hard data on use of and spending on a broad range of promotional vehicles, including direct mail, Web ads and Website sponsorships, email broadcasts, blog monitoring, search engine placement enhancement, newspaper and magazine ads, billboards, television and radio advertising, Website development and other forms of advertising.

The study also presents findings on use of and spending by colleges on marketing consultants such as market research agencies, public relations firms and advertising agencies, among others. In addition, the report explores the management and organization of the college's branding and promotional efforts, exploring the degree of centralization and other issues in the management of the college marketing effort.

TRENDS IN TRAINING COLLEGE FACULTY, STUDENTS & STAFF IN COMPUTER LITERACY
ISBN: 1-57440-085-1   Price: $67.50   Publication Date: April 2007

This report looks closely at how nine institutions of higher education are approaching the question of training faculty, staff and students in the use of educationally oriented information technologies. The report helps answer questions such as: what is the most productive way to help faculty master new information technologies? How much should be spent on such training? What are the best practices? How should distance learning instructors be trained? How formal, and how ad-hoc, should training efforts be? What should be computer literacy standards among students? How can subject-specific computer literacy be integrated into curriculums? Should colleges develop their own training methods, buy packaged solutions, find them on the Web?

Organizations profiled include: Brooklyn Law School, Florida State University College of Medicine, Indiana University Southeast, Texas Christian University, Clemson University, the Teaching & Learning Technology Group, the Appalachian College Association, Tuskegee Institute and the University of West Georgia.

THE SURVEY OF LIBRARY DATABASE LICENSING PRACTICES
ISBN: 1-57440-093-2   Price: $80.00   Publication Date: December 2007

The study presents data from 90 libraries – corporate, legal, college, public, state, and nonprofit libraries – about their database licensing practices. More than half of the participating libraries are from the U.S., and the rest are from Canada, Australia, the U.K., and other countries. Data are broken out by type and size of library, as well as for overall level of database expenditure. The 100+-page study, with more than 400 tables and charts, presents benchmarking data enabling librarians to compare their library's practices to peers in many areas related to licensing. Metrics provided include: percentage of licenses from consortiums, spending on consortium dues, time spent seeking new consortium partners, number of consortium memberships maintained; growth rate in the percentage of licenses obtained through consortiums; expectation for consortium purchases in the future; number of licenses, growth rate in the number of licenses, spending on licenses for directories, electronic journals, ebooks, and magazine/newspaper databases; future spending plans on all of the above; price inflation experienced for electronic resources in business, medical, humanities, financial, market research, social sciences and many other information categories; price inflation for ebooks, electronic directories, journals and newspaper/magazine databases; percentage of licenses that require passwords; percentage of licenses that have simultaneous access restrictions; spending on legal services related to licenses; and much more.

THE INTERNATIONAL SURVEY OF INSTITUTIONAL DIGITAL REPOSITORIES
ISBN: 1-57440-090-8   Price: $89.50   Publication Date: November 2007

The study presents data from 56 institutional digital repositories from 11 countries, including the U.S., Canada, Australia, Germany, South Africa, India, Turkey and other countries. The 121-page study presents more than 300 tables of data and commentary and is based on data from higher education libraries and other institutions involved in institutional digital repository development. In more than 300 tables and associated commentary, the report describes norms and benchmarks for budgets, software use, manpower needs and deployment, financing, usage, marketing and other facets of the management of international digital repositories. The report helps to answer questions such as: who contributes to the repositories and on what terms? Who uses the repositories? What do they contain and how fast are they growing in terms of content and end use? What measures have repositories used to gain faculty and other researcher participation? How successful have these methods been? How has the repository been marketed and cataloged? What has been the financial impact? Data are broken out by size and type of institution for easier benchmarking.

ACADEMIC LIBRARY WEBSITE BENCHMARKS
ISBN: 1-57440-094-0   Price: $85.00   Publication Date: January 2008

This report is based on data from more than 80 academic libraries in the U.S. and Canada. The 125+-page study presents detailed data on the composition of the academic library Web staff, relations with the college and library information technology departments, use of consultants and freelancers, budgets, future plans, Website marketing methods, Website revision plans, usage statistics, use of software, development of federated search and online forms and much more. Data are broken out by enrollment size, public and private status, Carnegie Class, as well as for libraries with or without their own Web staff.

PREVAILING & BEST PRACTICES IN ELECTRONIC AND PRINT SERIALS MANAGEMENT
ISBN: 1- 57440-076-2   Price: $80.00   Publication Date: November 2005

This report looks closely at the electronic and print serials procurement and management practices of 11 libraries, including: the University of Ohio, Villanova University, the Colorado School of Mines, Carleton College, Northwestern University, Baylor University, Princeton University, the University of Pennsylvania, the University of San Francisco, Embry-Riddle Aeronautical University and the University of Nebraska Medical Center. The report looks at both electronic and print serials and includes discussions of the following issues: selection and management of serials agents, including the negotiation of payment; allocating the serials budget by department; resolving access issues with publishers; use of consortiums in journal licensing; invoice reconciliation and payment; periodicals binding, claims, check-in and management; serials department staff size and range of responsibilities; serials management software; use of open access archives and university depositories; policies on gift subscriptions, free trials and academic exchanges of publications; use of electronic serials/catalog linking technology; acquisition of usage statistics; cooperative arrangements with other local libraries and other issues in serials management.

CREATING THE DIGITAL ART LIBRARY
Price: $80.00   Publication Date: October 2005

This special report looks at the efforts of 10 leading art libraries and image collections to digitize their holdings. The study reports on the efforts of the National Gallery of Canada, Cornell University's Knight Resource Center, the University of North Carolina, Chapel Hill; the Smithsonian Institution Libraries, the Illinois Institute of Technology, the National Archives and Records Administration, McGill University, Ohio State University, the Cleveland Museum of Art, and the joint effort of Harvard, Princeton, the University of California, San Diego, the University of Minnesota and others to develop a union catalog for cultural objects.

Among the issues covered: cost of outsourcing, cost of in-house conversions, the future of 35mm slides and related equipment, use of ARTstor and other commercial services, ease of interlibrary loan in images and the creation of a union catalog, prioritizing holdings for digitization, relationship of art libraries to departmental image collections, marketing image collections, range of end-users of image collections, determining levels of access to the collection, digitization and distribution of backup materials on artists lives and times, equipment selection, copyright, and other issues in the creation and maintenance of digital art libraries.

TRENDS IN MANAGEMENT OF LIBRARY SPECIAL COLLECTIONS IN FILM AND PHOTOGRAPHY
ISBN: 1-57440-001-01   Price: $80.00:   Publication Date: October 2005

This special report looks at the management and development of America's thriving special collections in film and photography. The report profiles the following collections: the University of Louisville, the Photographic Archives, the University of Utah's Multimedia Collection, The American Institute of Physics' Emilio Segre Visual Archives, the Newsfilm Library at the University of South Carolina, the University of California, Berkeley Pacific Film Archive; the UCLA Film and Television Archive, the Vanderbilt University Television News Archive, the National Archives and Records Administration's Special Media Preservation Laboratory; the University of Washington's Digital Initiatives.

The report covers digitization of photographs and film, special collection marketing, collection procurement, funding and financing, approaches for optimizing both sales revenues and educational uses, development of Web-based sale and distribution systems for photography and film, systems to assure copyright compliance, the development of online searchable databases, and many other aspects of film and photography special collections management.

THE MARKETING OF HISTORIC SITES, MUSEUMS, EXHIBITS AND ARCHIVES
ISBN: 1-57440-074-6   Price: $95.00   Publication Date: June 2005

This report looks closely at how history is presented and marketed by organizations such as history museums, libraries, historical societies, and historic sites and monuments. The report profiles the efforts of the Vermont Historical Society, Hook's Historic Drug Store and Pharmacy, the Thomas Jefferson Foundation/Monticello, the Musee Conti Wax Museum of New Orleans, the Bostonian Society, the Dittrick Medical History Center, the Band Museum, the Belmont Mansion, the Kansas State Historical Society, the Computer History Museum, the Atari Virtual Museum, the Museum of American Financial History, the Atlanta History Center and the public libraries of Denver and Evansville. The study's revealing profiles, based on extensive interviews with executive directors and marketing managers of the institutions cited, provide a deeply detailed look at how history museums, sites, societies and monuments are marketing themselves.

LICENSING AND COPYRIGHT MANAGEMENT: BEST PRACTICES OF COLLEGE, SPECIAL, AND RESEARCH LIBRARIES
ISBN: 1-57440-068-1   Price: $80   Publication Date: May 2004

This report looks closely at the licensing and copyright-management strategies of a sample of leading research, college and special libraries and consortiums and includes interviews with leading experts. The focus is on electronic-database licensing, and includes discussions of the most pressing issues: development of consortiums and group buying initiatives, terms of access, liability for infringement, archiving, training and development, free-trial periods, contract language, contract-management software and time-management issues, acquiring and using usage statistics, elimination of duplication, enhancement of bargaining power, open-access publishing policies, interruption-of-service contingency arrangements, changes in pricing over the life of the contract, interlibrary loan of electronic files, copyright clearance, negotiating tactics, uses of consortiums, and many other issues. The report profiles the emergence of consortiums and group-buying arrangements.

CREATING THE DIGITAL ACADEMIC LIBRARY
ISBN: 1-57440-071-1   Price: $69.50   Publication Date: July 2004

This report looks closely at the efforts of more than 10 major academic libraries to develop their digital assets and deal with problems in the area of librarian time management, database selection, vendor relations, contract negotiation and tracking, electronic-resources funding and marketing, technical development, archival access, open access publishing agit prop, use of ebooks, digitization of audio and image collections and other areas of the development of the digital academic library. The report includes profiles of Columbia University School of Medicine, the Health Sciences Complex of the University of Texas, Duke University Law Library, the University of Indiana Law Library, the University of South Carolina, the University of Idaho, and many others.

THE SURVEY OF LIBRARY CAFÉS
ISBN: 1-57440-089-4   Price: $75.00   Publication Date: 2007

The Survey of Library Cafés presents data from more than 40 academic and public libraries about their cafés and other foodservice operations. The 60-page report gives extensive data and commentary on library café sales volume, best-selling products, impacts on library maintenance costs, reasons for starting a café, effects on library traffic, and many other issues regarding the decision to start and manage a library café.

CORPORATE LIBRARY BENCHMARKS, 2007 Edition
ISBN: 1-57440-084-3   Price: $189.00

This report, our sixth survey of corporate libraries, presents a broad range of data, broken out by size and type of organization. Among the issues covered are: spending trends on books, magazines, journals, databases, CD-ROMs, directories and other information vehicles, plans to augment or reduce the scope and size of the corporate library, hiring plans, salary spending and personnel use, librarian research priorities by type of subject matter, policies on information literacy and library education, library relations with management, budget trends, breakdown in spending by the library versus other corporate departments that procure information, librarian use of blogs and RSS feeds, level of discounts received from book jobbers, use of subscription agents, and other issues of concern to corporate and other business librarians.

EMERGING ISSUES IN ACADEMIC LIBRARY CATALOGING & TECHNICAL SERVICES
ISBN: 1-57440-086-X   Price: $72.50   Publication Date: April 2007

This report presents nine highly detailed case studies of leading university cataloging and technical service departments. It provides insights into how they are handling 10 major changes facing them, including: the encouragement of cataloging productivity; impact of new technologies on and enhancement of online catalogs; the transition to metadata standards; the cataloging of Websites and digital and other special collections; library catalog and metadata training; database maintenance, holdings, and physical processing; managing the relationship with acquisitions departments; staff education; and other important issues. Survey participants represent academic libraries of varying sizes and classifications, with many different viewpoints. Universities surveyed are: Brigham Young; Curry College; Haverford College; Illinois, Louisiana and Pennsylvania State Universities; University of North Dakota; University of Washington; and Yale University.

EMERGING BEST PRACTICES IN LEGAL RECORDS MANAGEMENT
Price: $295.00   Publication Date: March 2006

This special report is based on detailed interviews with records managers, practice management directors and partners in major law firms and other legal offices. Among the organizational participants are: Kaye Scholer, Fulbright & Jawarski, Kilpatrick Stockton, Thomas Cooley Law School, the National Archives & Records Administration, Thompson Hine, Dewey Ballantine and Blackwell Sanders Peper Martin.

Among the issues covered in detail: Records Department Staff Size, Budget & Range of Responsibilities, Breakdown of Employee Time Use, Space Benchmarks for Offsite storage, Classification Scheme and Planning for Records Retrieval, Integration of Records with Copyright Information, Emails, Correspondence and other Forms of Legal Information, Types of Knowledge Management Software/Systems Under Consideration, Uses of Records Request Tracking, Strategies for Employee and Attorney Training in Content Control, USE of RFID & Barcoding Technology, Pace & Cost of Records Digitization, Digitization Technology & Storage Options, Records Security & Password Strategy, Relations Among the Library, Docket, Records Department, Information Technology Department and other Units Involved in Content/Knowledge Management and much more.

CORPORATE LIBRARY BENCHMARKS, 2005 EDITION
Price: $159.50   PDF Price: $174.50   Publication Date: October 2004
Corporate Library Benchmarks presents data from a survey of 50 major corporate and other business libraries. In more than 185 tables of data and commentary, the report charts developments in materials purchasing, use of office space, trends in use of librarian staff time, Fate of the physical library, trends in number of visitors to the library, trends in budgets, use of digital resources, role in knowledge management and many other facets of corporate librarianship. Data are broken out by major industry sector and by company size. Data contributed by many of America's leading corporations.

THE SURVEY OF LAW FIRM eMARKETING PRACTICES
Price: $295.00   Number of Tables: 120+
This study is based on a survey of 40 law firms with a mean size of 211 lawyers; data is broken out by size of law firm (by number of total lawyers) and by number of practice groups. Some data are also presented on a per-partner basis, such as spending on Website development per partner. In each firm a major marketing official answered questions regarding editorial staff, Website development and marketing, use of blogs, listservs, eNewsletters and other cyberspace promotional and information vehicles.

The report presents hard data on the use of search engine placement consultants, click-through rates on eNewsletters, number of unique visitors to the firm Website, and presents data on law firm spending plans for a broad range of eMarketing vehicles. The report presents hard data on law firm use of opt-in email, banner ads, Website sponsorship, per-click payments to Google, Yahoo, MSN and Overture, and much more.

The study also discusses the impact of Web-based press release distribution services and presents data on the number of law firms that use and plan to use such services. In addition to examining the prevailing methods of eMarketing, the report looks at law firm intentions in emerging eMarketing methods such as podcasting, Webcasting and streaming video, among others. The report presents quantitative assessment data on the usefulness of specific online directory sites such as Law.com, Findlaw.com and Superpages.com.

LAW LIBRARY BENCHMARKS, 2006-07 Edition
Price: $119.50   Publication Date: April 2006
Data are broken out for law firm, university law school, and public sector law libraries. Some data are also broken out for corporate law departments. The report provides data from more than 80 major law libraries and covers subjects such as staff size and growth, salaries and budget, spending trends in the library content budget, use of blogs, listservs and RSS feeds, spending on databases and commercial online services, use of and plans for CD-ROM, parent organization management's view of the future of the law library, assessment of attorney search skills, trends in information literacy training, use of reference tracking software, and much more.

Survey of Assessment Practices in Higher Education